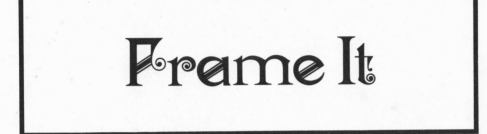

Frame It

Frame It

A Complete Do-It-Yourself Guide to Picture Framing

Lista Duren

HOUGHTON MIFFLIN COMPANY

BOSTON

To Rhoda, Jim, and Lark

Special thanks to Mrs. Marjorie Cohn for sharing her time and expertise.

Thank you to all the people at Frameworks in Cambridge, Massachusetts, and at the Frame Game Galleria in Jacksonville, Florida.

Thank you to Frances Tenenbaum.

Thank you to all the people whose pictures and frames appear on the following pages.

And thank you to Billy and Joanne for very special energies and cups of tea.

Designed by Joseph Weiler

Library of Congress Cataloging in Publication Data

Duren, Lista.   Frame it.

1.   Picture frames and framing.   I.   Title.
N8550.D87   749'.7   76-26666
ISBN 0-395-24765-9
ISBN 0-395-24976-7 pbk.

Printed in the United States of America

Contents

CONTENTS

Introduction

WHERE TO START when you know nothing about picture framing? Start by looking — casually and unhurriedly. Look at pictures in museums and offices and galleries and the homes of friends. Look at frames. See what they're made of and how they're finished and how the frame is shaped.

Look at mats. Notice the colors and the textures, the very wide ones and the very narrow ones, the ones with painted lines or designs on them, the ones covered with fabric.

Look at pictures with simple frames, with frames within frames, with huge ornate frames, and with no frames at all.

Now look at the artwork you want to frame. What are the outstanding characteristics of the piece? Subtle colors? Fine linework? Shiny surfaces? Big bold forms? How do you want the whole thing to look when you finish? Warm? Fragile? Bold? Modern? Playful? Keep these things in mind.

As with learning any new craft, framing will go more smoothly if you start with something simple, learn a little at a time, and work slowly. For your first framing project, choose something small. Large frames are clumsy and take longer to assemble. Unless you are skilled at using the tools already, I recommend buying your materials already cut to size for your first frame. Cutting mats, glass, and moldings takes practice and the cutting procedures will make more sense to you after you know how a frame is assembled.

Allow yourself plenty of time to frame something. It may take only half an hour to assemble a metal frame kit or a clip-on frame. It may take a whole afternoon to build a wooden frame. And it will take even longer if you are finishing your own molding, building a shadow box, covering a mat with fabric, or adding other special touches. Framing is a craft and it is important not to hurry if you want good results.

Good picture framing, though, is more than a matter of mastering techniques. There are practical and aesthetic reasons for selecting one framing process over another. First you must decide how much protection the art needs — are you framing an inexpensive print or a picture of sentimental or intrinsic value that you want to preserve? If it is the former, there are many options open to you, but if it is the latter, you will want the protection of archival framing and this will dictate the kinds of materials you must use.

You will find all of this basic information in Part One of this book, along with suggestions for framing a dozen different kinds of art — original graphics, watercolors, pastels and charcoal, rubbings, diplomas and other official papers, photographs, acrylic and oil paintings, fabric and needlework, tapestries and weavings, mosaics and stained glass, three-dimensional objects, and oversized pictures. Even if you are never to frame a picture yourself, this information will be helpful when you take something to be framed professionally.

Part Two is the heart of the craft of framing. Here you will find detailed information about materials and tools and where to get them. (No expensive or complicated tools are necessary.) In this section, too, you will learn how to cut all of the components of the different kinds of frames and how to assemble them.

Part Three consists of step-by-step instructions for building the frames described in the first part of the book. These instructions tell you exactly which of the techniques in Part Two you will be using, and then the exact order in which to assemble the parts of the frame. From my experience in helping novice framers, I have found that this arrangement of the material makes it possible to put together even your first frame without difficulty.

Part Four contains information and tips about hanging and displaying artwork. It also offers directions for making a standing frame if you don't want to hang a picture on a wall.

Throughout the text, suppliers for needed materials are identified. Addresses for these suppliers are listed under "Sources" at the back of the book.

Choosing a Frame

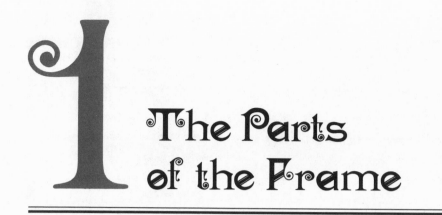

The Parts of the Frame

WHEN YOU CHOOSE your materials, remember that the purpose of framing is to present a work of art to its best advantage, and also to protect it against a multitude of dangers. Archival framing is the term that refers to framing in which precautions are taken to preserve the art in its original state. It is discussed in detail in Chapter 2. Be sure to read it carefully if you are framing anything that has value or may have value in the future.

The following is a brief description of the components of a frame and what they do, and some aesthetic criteria for choosing them.

GLASS AND BACKING   The art, whatever it is, must be held flat for viewing because bulges and wrinkles are distracting. So fabric is stretched on a rigid backing, and paper is held in place between glass on the front and stiff cardboard or Fome-Cor on the back. Paper that is framed without glass is likely to ripple or bulge. In addition to keeping the work flat, glass keeps it clean and protects it from damage. Glass is not used for paintings on wood or canvas, for the paint has its own protective shield. Glass may be used over fabric or needlework.

Wood frame for artwork on paper

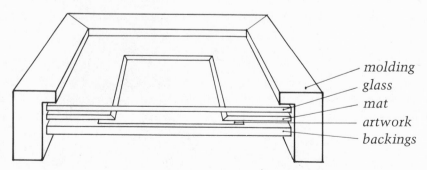

molding
glass
mat
artwork
backings

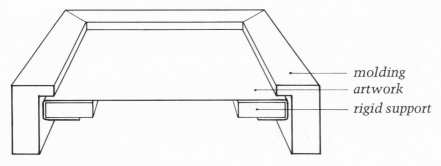

Wood frame for fabric or paintings on canvas

MATS If artwork is framed in contact with glass, condensation on the inner surface of the glass may cause waterspotting, mold growth, or rot, so a mat, a cardboard border, is used to create a space between the glass and the artwork. Mats are used primarily with artwork on paper. (If you are framing fabric with glass, or paper artwork that doesn't look right with a mat, you can use spacers — very thin strips of wood or mat board, invisible from the front of the frame — to separate the glass from the art.)

The mat serves a visual purpose too. It provides space around the art so that it doesn't appear crowded by the frame. And a mat can also be decorative. It can be painted or covered with fabric or combined with other mats.

Most mats and stiff backing boards are made of wood pulp, which has an acid content that will hasten the aging of the artwork. Acid-free rag board mats provide the best possible protection for your artwork. You should also use rag board or rag paper immediately behind the artwork if you want to protect the picture from acid in the stiff backing.

Mat Color A mat will emphasize its own color in a picture; a red mat will call attention to the red areas, a blue one to the blue areas, and so forth. Sometimes it is beneficial to emphasize certain areas of the artwork in this way, but in other cases, especially when the picture contains several areas of pure color, emphasis on one color will completely distort the artist's composition.

The color of the mat can in many instances determine the predominant tone of the framed picture — whether it will appear warm or cool, calm or lively. Always try both light-colored samples and dark ones. A dark color may overpower a light, fragile drawing, or it may provide just the right contrast to pop it out and focus your attention on it. A dark mat will generally seem to enclose the picture, while a light mat of the same size will appear more expansive.

3

When you choose a mat color, remember that colors react with each other — the same color may appear completely different when viewed next to two different colors. A mat may appear gray by itself, but when you hold it next to the picture, it may be brown or green or purple. Also remember that all colors change in different lighting. Always try a sample of the mat color next to the artwork before buying it, and observe the lighting situation where you are choosing the mat. If the lights there are fluorescent and you plan to display the picture under incandescent light, try to view the mat next to the picture in incandescent light before buying it.

Mat Size There is no standard mat size. Most mats are from 1½" to 3½" wide. Anything narrower than 1½" is considered a small mat, and anything wider than 3½" is considered a large one.

Keep in mind the visual reason for the mat — to isolate the artwork and allow the viewer to focus on it more easily. If your artwork is very small, a wide mat, even as wide as 4" or 5" all around, can be quite effective in drawing the viewer's attention to the art and providing a neutral area in which it can be viewed without distraction. A small mat and frame on a small picture can easily become lost, especially on a busy wall.

A large mat usually looks best with a wide frame. However, there are times when a wide frame looks good with a very thin mat. You should almost always avoid making the mat and the frame the same size, since it sets up a rhythm that can distract attention from the picture (although I have seen even this done successfully).

As you will learn later, if you want the mat to appear to be the same size all around, you will have to make the bottom border slightly larger. Some people prefer to make the mat noticeably larger on the bottom than on the top and sides.

Sometimes you will want to alter the orthodox proportions of the mat. You may want to make the sides very narrow in proportion to the top and bottom to accentuate the verticality of the artwork, or make the sides very wide to accentuate the horizontality. Or you may want to use a mat to change the proportions of a print so that it will fit in a frame you already have.

The color of the mat will usually influence how large you want it to be. A large mat of a bright color could be overpowering (although in some situations it will be appropriate), while a thin mat of the same color might provide just the right accent.

4 **FRAMES** The frame encloses and supports the art, mat, glass, and backing. The frame may be wood or metal or a minimal system of clips that hold the glass and backing together in only a few places. Wood and metal frames can be sealed to protect the art against dust and insects.

The major requirement of a frame is that it should call attention to the item being framed, not to itself. It is easy to overpower a picture with a strong mat color or an elaborate frame, or to choose a frame style that appeals to you or matches your decor but is not compatible with the artwork. Remember that framing should make viewing the art easier by allowing you to focus your attention on it without being distracted by the pattern of the wallpaper or an overly ornate molding. Framing should provide an area where only that piece of art exists and where it is all-important.

A very small serigraph by Charlotte Taft is framed with a very wide mat and a carved wooden frame. The window of the mat is cut large enough so that the uneven edges of the print are visible.

Choosing a framing technique that works visually is a design problem. The best way to approach it is to experiment with samples of moldings, mats, or backgrounds, and notice how each one affects the appearance of the piece you are framing. Try every sample that looks interesting, even if it doesn't seem like a likely solution. If it doesn't work, it may lead to more ideas.

One way to alter mat margins for a special effect. This reproduction of a painting by the impressionist Pissarro is horizontal but is matted to fit a vertical frame. The picture is framed with a gold frame and a double mat. The thin band of white mat next to the picture emphasizes the light, airy quality of the painting and keeps it from seeming enclosed or restricted by the larger brown mat. The original is in the Louvre.

The following are several points to be considered when deciding which frames look best with the artwork:

Sense of Enclosure   The way a picture is framed can determine whether it appears to be enclosed and separate from the surrounding space, or whether it flows with no obstruction and becomes part of the surrounding area, or whether it seems to be floating in a space of its own. A molding that projects forward from the picture will appear to enclose it more than one in which the picture sits almost flush with the front face of the molding. A strong color will usually provide more of a sense of enclosure than a neutral color; a wide frame is more prominent and therefore bounds the picture more noticeably than a small frame. A frame that slants inward toward the picture suggests enclosure more than the same width frame sloping back toward the wall. A large frame, a prominent band of color, a frame that physically projects forward from the picture, all act to stop the movement of the eye, to turn it back inward to the artwork. A lack of frame and a continuum of related colors, on the other hand, present no visual obstruction.

Many pictures require a sense of enclosure, but others, especially brightly colored modern art posters, make a strong enough statement by themselves — a very thin border or no border at all is sufficient to set them off visually.

Visual Weight   The visual weight has nothing to do with how much the picture actually weighs. It refers to how heavy the picture appears to be. Dark colors and strong lines will make a picture appear heavier than one with light colors or fragile linework. Certainly you have seen pictures where the frame looked much too heavy or too skimpy and thus detracted from the artwork. In general a deep or wide frame looks heavier than a narrow one; a bright color usually has more visual weight than a neutral one; and a closely framed picture often appears heavier than one with a wide mat that provides ample space between picture and frame.

Visual Qualities of the Artwork   The artwork itself can tell you a lot about what kind of frame will look best with it. An interior scene or picture with a sense of perspective will usually be enhanced by a frame that projects from the picture surface and adds to the feeling of depth. A piece that appears to be all on one plane will probably look best in a flat simple frame. If the work of art is dominated by sharp edges and angular lines, try an angular frame; if the forms are soft and curvilinear, try a frame with a curved profile. Most impressionist

7

paintings would be stifled in dark heavy frames, but delicate white or gold frames will enhance their soft light and bright color. A piece of art with an antique appearance demands an antique-looking frame, a print with a childlike quality should be framed with that in mind, and so on. Look at the piece you are framing and verbalize your immediate feelings about it. Then try to find a frame that suits your description.

When you are agonizing over which frame to use or how big to make the mat, remember that if you really don't like it after living with it for a while, you can always change your mind and reframe it another way. In fact it's not a bad idea to consider reframing a piece occasionally. Changing the frame or mat may give you a completely new perspective on a piece of art that you've had around for a long time. And the frame that you take off one picture now, given a new coat of paint, may be just right for another one. So don't feel trapped by today's decisions — framing doesn't have to be forever.

Archival Framing

THE TERM ARCHIVAL framing refers to the entire process of framing in which every precaution is taken to preserve the artwork in its original state. In archival framing you must use certain materials and follow specific procedures to guard against present or future damage to the artwork. Since every framing problem is different, there is not a set list of archival procedures. Instead the framer should familiarize himself with the conditions that can be harmful to art and take whatever steps are appropriate.

Archival framing can be expensive and time consuming, so for each piece you frame you should decide which archival measures are appropriate, based on how valuable the piece is, how fragile it is, and how long you want it to last.

For example: If you are framing an inexpensive poster to brighten up a room, and you will probably replace it within a year or two with something else, you may decide not to use acid-free framing materials. However, you probably will want to put glass over it to keep it from warping or getting dirty.

If you are framing a child's drawing on inferior quality paper, or anything else of sentimental value, and you want it to last for several years, you will probably want to use acid-free materials to extend its life.

If the piece you are framing is an original or valuable piece of art, you will want to use acid-free materials, make sure it is not framed in contact with the glass, and carefully consider where to hang it so that it will be least affected by environmental conditions.

If the piece is not only valuable but very old and fragile, you may want to take further measures to preserve it, such as using a special ultraviolet-filtering acrylic rather than regular glass, or hanging a cloth over the front of the frame which can be lifted for viewing.

CONDITIONS HARMFUL TO ARTWORK
Sunlight Sunlight fades colors of paper, paint, or fabric. Textile dyes

are especially sensitive to light. Any light causes fading — direct sun, reflected sunlight, and artificial light. The ultraviolet rays present in both natural and fluorescent light also accelerate fading and hasten deterioration.

To protect against the effects of light, pictures should never be hung in direct sunlight or directly opposite a window. Pictures which are especially sensitive to light can be hung in a room that receives very little light, or a fabric covering may be hung over the front of the picture and removed for viewing. A common practice is to rotate pictures occasionally from room to room so that no piece is constantly exposed to harsh lighting conditions.

If the piece is extremely valuable, you can use a special acrylic that filters out ultraviolet light in place of ordinary glass or acrylic. Trade names for this product are Plexiglas UF-3 made by Rohm and Haas, and Acrylite OP-3 made by American Cyanamid. You can mail order it from Talas or your local plastics dealer can order it, but there may be minimum order requirements and it will be expensive.

You can also purchase ultraviolet filtering covers for fluorescent tubing. Check with your local fluorescent light dealer.

Humidity   Artwork responds drastically to extreme humidity or dryness. Very dry air causes the paper to become dry and brittle, and excessive humidity is likely to cause waterspotting, mildewing, and mold growth. Damage may also occur when changes in the relative humidity between the atmosphere inside the frame and the atmosphere in the surrounding room cause moisture to condense on the inside surface of the glass. Photographic emulsion is a particularly favorable environment for mold growth, which can cause the photograph to adhere to the glass. Mold also feeds readily on pastels.

A mat should be used to lift the glass away from the artwork so that if there is condensation inside the frame it will be less likely to damage the artwork. Spacers may be used if a mat is not desirable.

Hang the picture in a dry place — not the kitchen or bathroom — and not near a window or on an exterior masonry wall, which may seep moisture.

Provide adequate air circulation around the picture. Put little cork or felt pads on the back of the frame at the bottom corners to lift it out from the wall so that air can circulate behind it. Don't store the artwork in a basement or an attic, or in any other place that does not have adequate ventilation.

Acrylic is a better thermal insulator than glass and therefore doesn't condense moisture so readily. It may be used for better protection against waterspotting and mold growth.

If mold growth does occur it is most likely to become visible as dull rust-colored patches called foxing, but it also occurs in a variety of other colors. If you notice any evidence of dampness or mold growth in a frame, remove the picture from the frame and place it in a dry environment where air can circulate freely. If discoloration remains, consult a professional conservator.

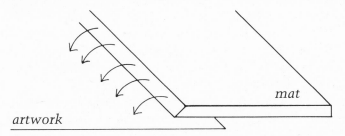

mat

artwork

Acids from the core of the mat board "breathe" onto the artwork.

Acid Acid is present in any wood or wood pulp product — this can be molding, mat board, cardboard, etc. If artwork is framed in acidic materials, it will become discolored and brittle in a period of several months to a few years. Discoloration from the mat appears as a brown line on the artwork just inside the opening of the mat; this is because the core of the mat board is more acidic than the surface and the acids "breathe" from the cut edge of the mat onto the artwork. Discoloration from corrugated cardboard backing appears as brown lines which correspond to the corrugations.

To protect the artwork from the effects of acid, use only acid-free framing materials in contact with the artwork. The mat and the backing immediately behind the artwork should both be acid-free. A nonporous barrier, Mylar or aluminum foil, can also be placed between the acid-free backing and the stiff backing to prevent any acid's traveling through to the artwork.

When fabric or paintings on canvas are to be stretched on an acidic backing, a sheet of acid-free rag board should be placed over the backing first, or the backing should be sealed with polyurethane.

Air Pollution and Dirt Sulfur dioxide from the air is absorbed by paper and converted to sulfuric acid. It makes the paper brittle and causes discoloration. This is more of a problem with inferior wood-pulp papers than with high-grade rag paper. Dust from the air settles on artwork just as it settles on everything else. You have only to clean the glass on the front of a picture to see how much dirt would actually be on the artwork if the glass weren't there.

11

Frame the artwork with acid-free rag board mat and backing. The acid-free board is chemically inert and won't react with gases in the air. Use glass or acrylic in the frame and seal the back of the frame to keep out dirt. Don't hang a picture in the path of an air vent.

Handling   Art is easily frayed, torn, wrinkled, or punctured by careless handling, and if not protected in some way it is subject to fingerprints, stains, and dust as well. If a picture is not being framed immediately, a mat and backing or an acid-free envelope, or both, will provide some protection. An acid-free envelope may be made of acid-free paper or Mylar. Some art supply stores carry them and you can mail order them from Talas.

Whenever you handle the artwork make sure you have clean hands. Work slowly and carefully. Use both hands to move artwork to avoid bending, creasing, or tearing the picture. Your hands exude oils that can stain the artwork or the mat, and sharp or stiff objects may scratch the surface of the artwork, so don't touch the surface of the picture with your fingers, tape measure, or anything else. Handle it only by the edges.

Heat   Heat accelerates the deterioration of the artwork and dries out wood molding, making it weaker and more likely to split. A picture should not be hung over a radiator or other source of heat, and molding for building a frame should not be stored next to a heat source. One of the worst places to hang a picture is over a fireplace; the artwork there can be affected not only by heat but by soot and gummy residues.

Insects   Silverfish, woodworms, termites, and roaches feed on frames, paper, glue, and sometimes even paint. Seal the back of the frame and check it periodically for traces of insects and to make sure the seal isn't broken.

Defects in the Paper   Artwork on poor quality paper will deteriorate much more rapidly than art on high quality paper. The addition of chemicals in the paper-making process sometimes leaves residues destructive to the paper. Foreign objects in the paper weaken it. And shorter fibers mean weaker paper. Chemically inert rag paper lasts much longer than acidic paper.

Abrasion   Paintings on stretched canvas are subject to abrasion in wooden moldings since the lip of the molding extends over the edge

12

of the canvas and gradually wears away the painted surface. To protect the painting, glue strips of felt to the underside of the lip before you put the painting into the frame.

PROTECTIVE MEASURES FOR ART ON PAPER

Glazing   Use a clear protective covering of glass or acrylic over the artwork to guard against dirt, air pollution, and handling. Ultraviolet-filtering Plexiglas will protect valuable pieces against ultraviolet rays. Acetate can be used as temporary protection for unframed pictures.

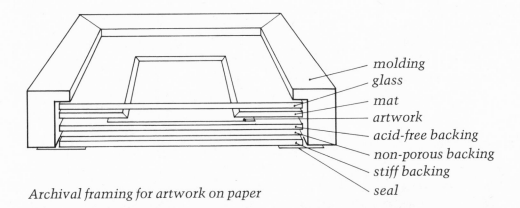

molding
glass
mat
artwork
acid-free backing
non-porous backing
stiff backing
seal

Archival framing for artwork on paper

Mat or Spacers   Glass or acrylic should not be in direct contact with artwork, since condensation trapped against the art can result in waterspotting or mold growth. Provide a space between glazing and artwork by using a mat or spacers.

Stiff Backing   The stiff backing behind the artwork prevents warping and protects against scratching, tearing, or puncturing from behind.

Acid-free Materials   Everything in contact with the artwork must be acid-free or chemically neutral, including the tape or glue that holds the artwork in place. The mat should be acid-free rag board or a neutralized wood pulp board. (All rag board is not acid-free; you can test it with an archivist's pen from Talas.) The backing immediately in contact with the artwork should be chemically inert rag board. Rubber cement, cellophane tape, or masking tape should never be used on artwork. Attach it with linen tape or archival paste and acid-free rice paper hinges.

13

Nonporous Backing A nonporous backing, aluminum foil or Mylar, should be inserted between the stiff backing and the acid-free backing so that acids cannot travel through to the artwork. Mylar is preferable since it does not condense moisture so easily as aluminum foil.

PROTECTIVE MEASURES FOR PAINTINGS

Padding Glue a strip of felt to the underside of the lip of the molding so that the frame does not scratch the surface of the painting.

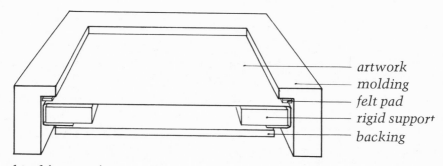

artwork
molding
felt pad
rigid support
backing

Archival framing for paintings on canvas

Fitting Wooden stretcher frames and wooden panels must have room to expand and contract within the frame, so the frame should fit loosely. The artwork should be held in place with metal plates instead of brads, since brads would not allow the wood to expand. The plates should be screwed into the molding and allowed to extend over the back of the artwork to hold it in place, but they should not be screwed into the art itself.

Backing Cardboard or Fome-Cor, a paper-coated polystyrene board, tacked onto the back of the stretcher protects against dirt and puncturing.

Dusting Your Paintings The frames of paintings should be dusted by vacuuming with a small brush attachment so that the dust isn't stirred up to resettle. The painting itself should be dusted with a lint-free cloth. Paintings should also be examined periodically in very strong light from one side for cracks in the surface — a dusting cloth may catch in the cracks and pull chips of paint from the surface. Paintings that are cracked or chipped should not be dusted. Instead consult an art conservator about proper measures for cleaning or restoring the artwork.

To find an art conservator in your area, call your local art museum.

Storage Stored pictures should be lifted off the floor to protect against the possibility of water damage. They should be stored vertically with some room between them to allow air to circulate. Artwork should not be stored in very damp or very dry places. Never allow anything to lean against a painting on canvas; the canvas stretches easily and a bulge is hard to remove.

FOR FUTURE REFERENCE

After you finish framing anything that is valuable or might become valuable, record on the back of the frame the procedures you have followed — whether or not acid-free materials were used, what glues or adhesives were used, what fixatives or other sprays you applied to the artwork, and whether or not the artwork has been cleaned or restored and what procedures were used. This information will be helpful if the artwork ever needs cleaning or restoring or reframing in the future. Anything recorded on the back of the frame should be in pencil. Ink fades and runs.

3 Minimal Display Methods

THE PROCEDURES IN this chapter require few materials and very little time. They also provide only minimal or short-term protection for the artwork. None of the methods includes a stiff backing or support. Although some do involve a clear protective covering, none offers the protection of glass or acrylic. Except for stretching, which can be a permanent display method, the other options are temporary — good for use in portfolios or sales displays, or for hanging posters or other art that you don't care to keep for more than a year or so.

MOUNTING Mounting is a process for sticking cloth or paper to a rigid backing using glue or dry mount tissue. It is a quick and inexpensive way to stiffen something for hanging and the rigid backing protects the artwork against tearing or fraying. Mounted artwork can be hung with or without a frame. It is an excellent method for a poster or map since it minimizes the appearance of fold lines and wrinkles.

Although mounting is often the only way to keep a warped print or photograph flat, it drastically reduces the value of any original piece of art, including photographs. Mounting is not considered an archival process because the artwork can't be removed from the backing and still be preserved in its original state. Therefore original or valuable artwork should not be mounted.

Mounted artwork without a protective covering is subject to dirt and stains, and is likely to warp to some degree unless it is framed with glass. If you are planning to put glass over the artwork, the glass will usually hold the paper flat, eliminating the need for mounting. However, even with glass, posters on thin paper sometimes start to ripple in a frame. Mounting will correct this condition.

Mounting is a permanent process in that the art can't be removed from the backing. However, you can add a mat, glass, frame, or all three to a mounted piece of art.

Dry Mounting Dry mounting is a heat process. The bonding agent

16

This reproduction of a drawing by Billy McDonald was wet mounted on Upson board and framed without glass in a natural walnut frame.

17

The Reluctant Dragon *was dry mounted onto a Fome-Cor backing larger than the poster. The backing and poster were trimmed to exactly the same size after mounting.* © *Portal Publications, Sausalito, Cal.*

18 is a sheet of mounting tissue that is covered on both sides with an adhesive activated by heat. Dry mounting requires the use of a dry

A reproduction of the painting Nachtliche Blumen *by Paul Klee was dry mounted on a Fome-Cor backing the same size as the outer dimension of the mat. The mat was attached to the backing with double-stick tape. The original painting is in the Wolfgang Museum, Essen, Germany.*

mount press — you might have access to one at a do-it-yourself frame shop, a photographic darkroom, or a university art or photography department. Very small items, smaller than 8″ x 10″, can be mounted at home with an iron.

Dry mounting is not foolproof. Pockets of air occasionally get trapped underneath the print, causing wrinkling, bubbling, or even tearing. So if the artwork is not replaceable, it should not be dry mounted.

Dry mounting takes about 20 minutes for something small and up to an hour and a half for something very large. Instructions are in Chapter 15.

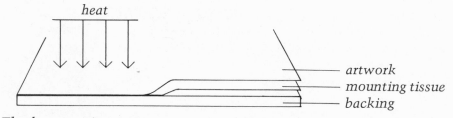

The dry mounting process

Wet Mounting In wet mounting, the artwork is fastened to the backing with a vegetable paste in a process similar to wallpapering. Wet mounting does not require any special equipment, but it is a messy job requiring a large work space. Because the mounting adhesive is noticeable at the edges of the paper, this method is not satisfactory if you intend to leave some of the backing showing as a border around the artwork.

Wet mounting takes 30 minutes to an hour and the mounted artwork must dry under a weight for several hours. Instructions are in Chapter 15.

Other Mounting Methods Spray adhesives can be used for mounting but my experience is that the spray always gets on something I didn't mean to spray it on, like the front of the artwork, and it doesn't really hold that well; it's also bad to breathe.

Positionable mounting adhesive is a sheet of paper coated on both sides with an adhesive that doesn't bond until you apply pressure. It comes in sheets up to 16″ x 20″. It is fairly easy to work with, holds well, does not require special equipment or heat, and is not messy like wet mounting or spray adhesive. It forms a permanent bond. Trade names are Scotch Positionable Mounting Adhesive, Falcon Perma/Mount, and Telesar Permanent Picture Mount. It is sold at photography stores and some art supply stores; you can also order it from Twin City Moulding and Supply.

The instructions are simple and come with the product.

LAMINATING If you prefer not to use glass or acrylic on a mounted item, you can apply a clear plastic laminate to the front. This is an ideal method of providing a protective coating over a poster to be hung in the kitchen or bathroom, since it won't fog up like glass will and it can be sponged clean. Laminates should never be applied to original or valuable artwork since they can't be removed.

A clear plastic laminate that adheres with heat is available. It mounts at about 300° F. and requires the use of a dry mount press. It is not safe to use on a poster that has been mounted on Fome-Cor because the temperature is high enough to melt the foam center of the board. Since the laminate is likely to bubble if it is applied to something that is already mounted, apply the laminate to the face of the poster first and *then* mount the poster and plastic laminate to a stiff backing.

After applying a laminate at the required high temperature, the dry mount press can't be used for regular dry mounting for a couple of hours — until it cools — so many people will allow their presses to be used for applying laminates only at specified times or not at all. Check before you go.

MAT AND BACKING Artwork on paper and stiff pieces of fabric or needlework may be temporarily displayed or protected by placing them between a mat and a stiff backing.

The mat and backing provide protection against fraying, tearing, bending, and puncturing. However, the surface of the artwork is not protected from scratches and dirt unless a protective covering is used over the mat. A mat and backing can be used in combination with acetate or shrinkwrapping. These are not satisfactory permanent measures, but for presentations, portfolios, or temporary display purposes they are fine. A mat will always make a piece of artwork look a little more finished and professional.

Instructions for cutting mats are given in Chapter 11. It takes practice to cut a good mat, but once you learn how it doesn't take long — 15 or 20 minutes for each mat.

ACETATE Thin sheets of clear acetate can be used as temporary protection for artwork, but since acetate scratches and tears easily and becomes brittle within a few months, it does not provide good permanent protection. Acetate is commonly used to cover artwork for sale or temporary display, or to protect artwork in storage or in a portfolio.

Acetate is easy to apply; it only takes about 15 minutes. For instructions, see Chapter 22.

SHRINKWRAPPING Shrinkwrapping is a method of tightly enclosing the artwork in very thin plastic to protect it against stains, dirt, and fraying. The artwork must have a stiff backing and it can also be matted. This is an excellent method of protecting the artwork temporarily; it is not permanent because the plastic is thin and easily punctured and torn. It is used in the same cases as acetate.

Shrinkwrapping requires a machine that is not generally available to the public, even in do-it-yourself frame stores. However, the

21

service is offered by a number of art supply and framing stores. Instructions are not included in this book.

STRETCHING   A painting on canvas or a piece of fabric or needlework should be stretched taut on a rigid backing to pull out all wrinkles and unevenness so that the image and texture may be enjoyed. A stretched piece may be hung with or without a frame, and it can be framed with or without glass.

Stretching isn't hard; it just requires some patience. The amount of time needed to stretch something varies with the size of the piece and the complexity of the problem. It usually takes about 45 minutes.

Complete instructions for stretching are in Chapter 16.

A brightly colored printed fabric stretched on a wood support and hung without a frame.

4 Frameless Frames

THESE ARE METHODS of displaying the artwork between glass or acrylic and a stiff backing without actually using a wood or metal frame. All of these frames are fairly quick to assemble — an hour or less. Any of them might be used to permanently display artwork, but archival quality framing is possible only with the passe-partout frame.

CLIP FRAMES   There are numerous clip systems on the market which are used as an alternative to the wooden frame. These systems clamp glass, mat, artwork, and backing together in 2 or more places.

The most widely available are:

Braquettes — Metal or plastic clips which hold the artwork at the top and bottom. The two clips are joined by a string.

Fast Frame — Plastic clips which secure the glass and backing at the four corners, and are joined by a string.

Uni-Frame — Two arms cross on the back near each corner to clip the artwork in eight places. The clips are joined by string. There are two sizes available — the Uni-Frame 20 to use on artwork less than 16″ x 20″ and the Uni-Frame 40 to use on pieces from 16″ x 20″ up to 40″ x 40″.

Eubank Frame — The same system as the Uni-Frame produced in stainless steel. It can be used on pieces from 16″ x 20″ up to 40″ x 40″.

Kulicke Strip Frame — A metal strip adjustable from 8″ to 45″ supports the artwork from behind with only very small clips visible from the front.

Clip systems are easily and quickly assembled at home. They offer you the protection of the glass and backing without building a wood frame. And they look quite good on modern art posters and prints. They do not allow you to seal the artwork against dust, however, so this would not qualify as archival framing. Since the edge of the glass is exposed it can easily chip or break, and you can cut yourself on a sharp edge.

Since the components are clipped together in only a few places rather than continuously, you may have a problem with the mat and backing warping away from the glass between the clips. (The systems which clip in eight places give the most support.) However, if this happens you can always remove the clips and build a wooden or metal frame instead. Clips are reusable even for something a different size or shape.

Clip frames are available at frame shops, galleries, museum shops, or art supply stores. The Uni-Frame and Eubank Frame can be ordered from Eubank Frame, Inc., if there is no supplier in your area.

A pen and ink drawing by Billy McDonald is matted and framed with glass and a Uniframe.

You can order the Kulicke Strip Frame from Kulicke. Braquettes and Fast Frames are available from Twin City Moulding and Supply.

Once you have cut all the materials it takes only a half hour or less to assemble the clip frame.

Instructions for assembly are in Chapter 23.

ACRYLIC BOX FRAMES Acrylic box frames are simply boxes with the back left open so that a slightly smaller cardboard box can slide in the back and hold the artwork snugly in place against the acrylic. These provide an excellent protective covering for the artwork with the added assurance that they are not breakable. But they scratch easily and they will melt if hung too near a heat source. They come only in standard sizes unless you want to construct your own. If you buy them ready-made, they are instant frames — all you do is pop the artwork in and cut a mat if you decide you want one. (Note: a mat for an acrylic box frame must be cut ¹⁄₁₆″ smaller in each direction than the opening in the box.) Acrylic is not cleaned the same way as glass. See Chapter 12 for cleaning instructions.

It will be cheaper to build your own box frame and you can make it exactly the size you want it. It takes a couple of hours. Instructions are in Chapter 24.

PASSE-PARTOUT FRAMES This is a very simple and interesting method for displaying some pieces of art. Glass and backing are held together at the edges with a paper or cloth tape of any color you like. A mat may be used if desired. It is possible to achieve archival quality framing with this method (if you use acid-free materials) since the edge of the frame is sealed.

The tape is not as sturdy as a wooden frame. It will begin to stretch with the weight of the glass and should be checked periodically and replaced before it gives way completely. If the picture you are framing is very large, consider using acrylic instead of glass because acrylic weighs less.

Passe-partout frames make the entire picture area appear extremely flat, so they generally work best with pictures that appear to be in one plane rather than pictures that have perspective.

Passe-partout is not difficult, but it requires some patience because it can be hard to apply the tape in a straight line. It will probably take about 45 minutes to an hour to assemble your first one.

Instructions are in Chapter 25.

25

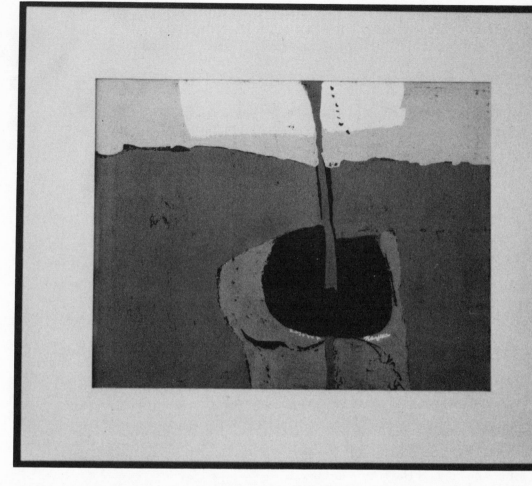

A passe-partout frame on a serigraph called Red Bud *by Japanese artist Kazuna Tanaka. The print is framed with glass and 100 percent rag board mat and backing.*

5 Metal and Wood Frames

THESE FRAMES PROVIDE a rigid wood or metal support around the edge of the artwork. Some can be used with a mat, glass, and/or backing. Others are intended for specific types of artwork or to solve specific framing problems. With the exception of the homemade metal frame these frames can be sealed from the back, and if archival quality materials are used and proper procedures are followed, you can achieve archival quality framing.

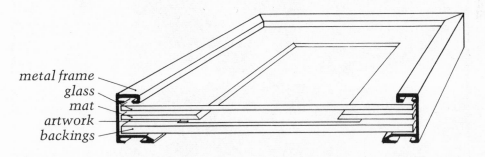

metal frame
glass
mat
artwork
backings

METAL SECTION FRAMES Metal section frames come in kits that are easily and quickly assembled at home with a screwdriver or an allen wrench. They come in two depths — one to accept artwork with mat, glass, and backing, and a deeper version to fit fabric on a stretcher frame. You can buy the kits at frame shops and art supply stores. Each package contains two sides of the frame, already cut, in lengths from 8″ to 40″. The pieces are precut only in 1″ increments — that is 8″, 9″, 10″, but not 8½″ or 9¾″. If the measurements of the piece you are framing are not whole numbers, you can mat it to a size that will fit a precut metal frame, or trim it, or find someone to cut the frame for you. Some frame shops will cut metal frames to order. These same shops may stock lengths longer than 40″.

Metal section frames are aluminum with a silver or gold ano-
dized finish or a baked-on acrylic finish in a variety of colors. There
are several brands; each one looks a little different, and some fit

The print V-3 by Tokio Miyashita, is framed with metal counter stripping, acrylic, 100 percent rag board mat and backing, and a wood stretcher frame in the back for stiffness. The mat window is cut large enough that the edge of the artwork and the artist's signature are visible.

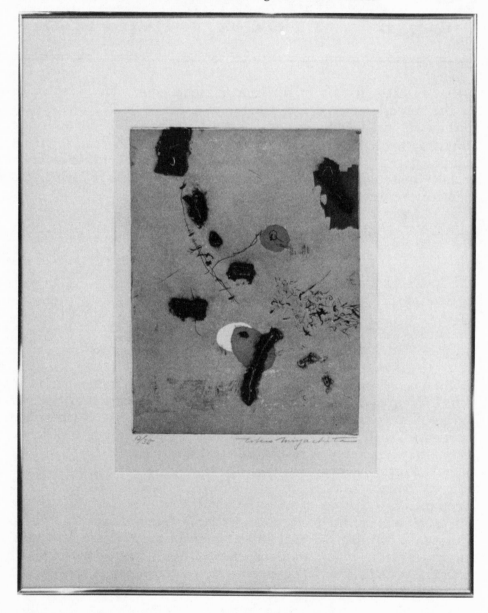

together better than others. I recommend Nielsen's frame called Framekit and the Kulicke Metal Section Frame.

Metal frames with the corners already joined are also available in department stores and art supply stores. They come in only a few standard sizes.

Once you have cut all the materials, metal section frames take about 45 minutes to assemble. Instructions are packaged with the frame pieces, and so are not included in this book.

HOMEMADE METAL FRAMES If you are not happy with the appearance or cost of metal frame kits, you can construct an inexpensive frame using aluminum counter molding from a hardware store and a wooden backing.

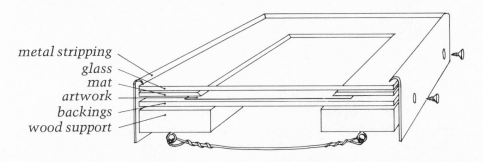

metal stripping
glass
mat
artwork
backings
wood support

This is not an easy frame to assemble, as there is practically no margin for error and it is difficult to cut the metal corners accurately, so I don't recommend this for the first frame you build. When you do try it, allow several hours to work on it, and purchase a little extra molding to practice on.

This frame is very heavy because of the wooden backing so you may want to use acrylic, which weighs less than glass.

Instructions for building your own metal frame are in Chapter 26.

STANDARD WOOD FRAME A wood frame starts out as a length of wood molding. You must cut the mitered corners, join the pieces together with glue and brads, and put the contents of the frame in place from the back. A standard wood molding has a lip — a projection on the front — that holds everything in place.

The wood frame provides a rigid support around the edge of the artwork and framing materials. It also provides protection from abrasion and dirt. It may be used for all kinds of artwork with or without glass or acrylic.

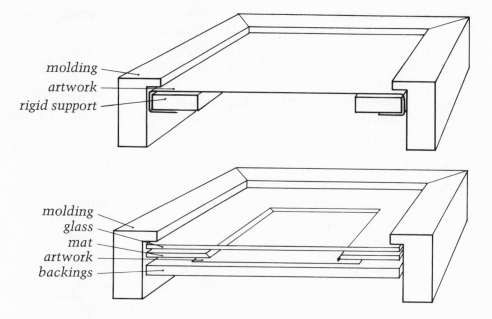

The molding for a wood frame may be very thin — ½″ or less — or it may be quite hefty — if you go to an art museum, you may see moldings as wide as 8″ or 10″. It may be very simple or very ornate. It may be painted, stained, metal leafed, or finished with clear materials that enhance the natural color and grain of the wood. In short, wood molding is extremely versatile; it is possible to achieve a wide range of effects by choosing wood moldings of different sizes, shapes, and finishes.

Depending on the complexity of the job, it may take anywhere from 2 hours to a whole afternoon to build a wood frame.

Instructions are in Chapter 27.

WOODEN FRAMES WITH LINERS A liner is a frame placed within another frame for decorative effect. Some liners serve the same purpose as a mat — to isolate the artwork and focus attention on it. These are usually fairly wide and simple in shape and painted

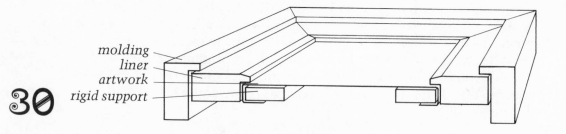

Painting Cathedrals *by Marjorie Masel, is framed in a simple walnut stained molding.*

or fabric-covered in white or neutral shades. Liners can also be used to make a frame more ornate or interesting. For this purpose the liner is often covered with metal leaf or brightly painted to contrast with the frame.

Building a frame with a liner is the same as building two frames for the same picture, and so takes about twice as long to build as a standard wooden frame.

Instructions are in Chapter 28.

31

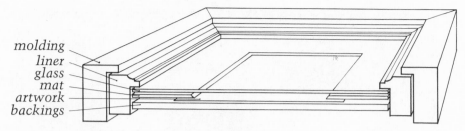

molding
liner
glass
mat
artwork
backings

Wood frame with liner for artwork on paper

SLAT FRAME   A slat frame is commonly called stripping because
it is simply a strip of wood with no lip. It may be purchased as lattice

*A small piece of oriental needlework is framed in a metal-leafed wood
frame with a red linen-covered liner and non-glare glass.*

32

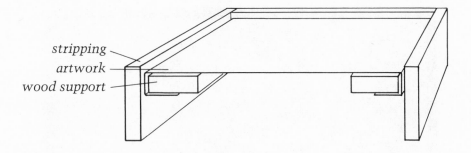

stripping
artwork
wood support

from a lumberyard or as finished stripping from a frame store. It is used only for artwork on a wood support or stretcher frame and is attached by nailing through the stripping into the wood support. Since the corners are not joined, this is a particularly good solution for framing out-of-square paintings. A slat frame can't be used with a mat or glass since there is no lip to hold the contents in place.

Stripping is usually about ¼" thick and about 1½" wide. It may be natural, stained, or painted, and the front edge is often finished with gold or silver paint or metal leaf.

Stripping may be attached to the picture so that the front (and thinnest) edge is flush with the face of the picture or so that the picture is recessed in the frame. Since there is no lip, the edges of the painting cannot be obscured or abraded by the frame.

The slat frame is the quickest of the wood frames to assemble. It usually takes less than an hour. Instructions are in Chapter 29.

FLOATER FRAMES The floater frame is another alternative for framing artwork on a wood support without glass or mat. Because of its simplified lines, it usually looks best on modern art. It has no lip. It is simply a strip of wood stepped in so that the painting rests on the bottom and innermost step and the front of the painting is flush with the front edge of the molding or slightly recessed. The front edge of the floater is usually painted or leafed, the outside edge painted or stained, and the inside edge painted black to make it appear that the art is floating in a dark space inside the frame.

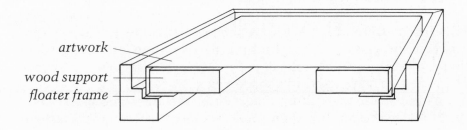

artwork
wood support
floater frame

33

Stained 1x2 fir was used as stripping for this large painting The Green Ones are Cannonballs, *by J. Lavy.*

A floater frame is fairly quick to build. Allow yourself an hour to an hour and a half.

Instructions are in Chapter 30.

SHADOW BOX FRAMES   A shadow box frame has a deep space between the glass and the backing to accommodate three-dimensional objects — dolls, folded paper compositions, string art, etc. There are two ways to build a shadow box.

You can use a molding made with two lips. The glass sits directly under the top lip; then there is a deep space and the artwork

This lively snapshot was enlarged to 8" x 10", mounted on a plywood backing, and framed with a floater frame.

sits against the bottom lip with the backing directly behind it.

But you don't need a double-lipped molding to build a shadow box. You can use any molding deep enough to accommodate the glass and backing and still leave enough room for the object you are framing. The procedure is to place the glass as usual against the lip of the molding, insert a spacer that holds the glass in place and provides a second lip, and then fasten the artwork and backing into place.

A shadow box usually isn't hard to build, but it will take several hours.

Instructions are in Chapter 31.

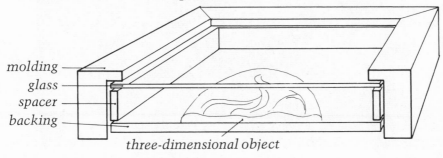

molding
glass
spacer
backing

three-dimensional object

35

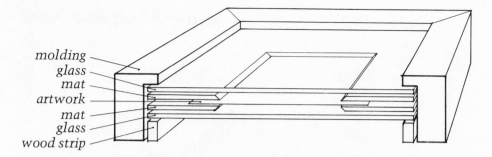

molding
glass
mat
artwork
mat
glass
wood strip

TWO-SIDED FRAMES   Occasionally you will have a piece of art or a document that you will want to frame so that both the front and the back can be viewed. You will therefore want to put a mat and glazing on both sides. There are two alternatives: you can frame the piece between two pieces of glass or acrylic with a wood molding (you can achieve archival framing if you use two acid-free mats and seal the frames); or you can put the artwork between two pieces of acrylic and fasten them together at the corners with rivets.

Instructions for both kinds of two-sided frame are in Chapter 32.

A map of the Holy Land framed between two pieces of acrylic which are drilled and held together by screw posts.

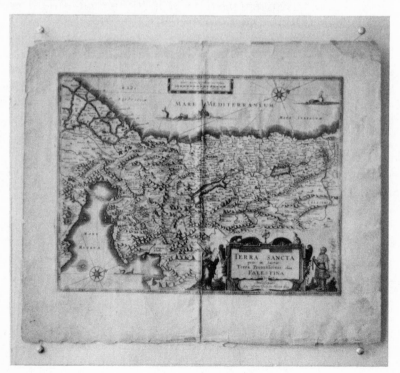

Mats

THE MAT IS THE MOST flexible of the framing components, with infinite possible combinations of size, color, proportion, painted decoration, surface texture, number and shape of windows, and combination with other mats. The mat is also a strong visual element in framing. A simple variation in the way a picture is matted can change the whole effect of the framed piece.

Instructions for cutting all the mats in this chapter appear in Chapter 11.

STANDARD MAT The standard mat is one piece of mat board with one opening cut in it. The opening is usually a little above the center of the mat. Most mats have a bevelled cut around the window, but some people prefer the appearance of a straight cut. You can do it either way.

If you can't find the color you need in mat board, you can purchase good quality colored paper and dry mount it to the face of a sheet of white mat board or rag board. Then cut the mat as you normally would. The papers I recommend are Color-Aid Paper, which has a flat surface of silk-screened color (the surface is beautiful but very easily scratched), Pantone paper, Canson paper, or Miliani Ingres Text paper. Art supply stores carry colored papers.

MULTIPLE WINDOW MATS Two or more openings can be cut in the same mat if you want to frame several pieces together. Items may be arranged vertically or horizontally, symmetrically or asymmetrically. Usually the composition will look more balanced if there is a wider mat at the bottom, and if the side margins are slightly larger than the space between openings. A good way to visualize a multiple window mat is to place the items being framed on a large piece of mat board the color you want and move the objects in relation to each other until you find a composition that pleases you. Lines of movement in the pictures may suggest the best arrange-

A collage with a simple mat.

ment. Groups of photographs are best arranged with the people in the photos facing toward the center of the framed composition.

MATS WITH CURVED WINDOWS Occasionally a round etching, an oval photograph, or some other unusual piece of art will require a mat with an oddly shaped window. Some frame shops have a machine for cutting curved windows, but with the help of a Dexter cutter, you will find that it isn't as hard as it looks to cut one yourself. In fact, a lot of people feel that it is easier to cut a curve than a straight line with a Dexter cutter. It is also possible to cut a curved

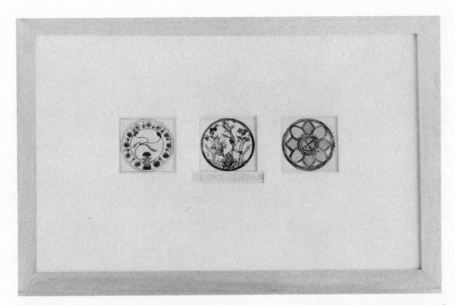

Three tiny watercolor drawings by Bernice Levenson are displayed with a white rag board mat with three windows. The middle window has been extended to include the artist's signature.

window by hand with a mat knife, but it's pretty difficult to keep the bevel constant and cut a smooth curve at the same time.

FABRIC-COVERED MATS A fabric-covered mat is often the answer when an ordinary mat looks too flat or too plain or just not right next to your artwork. Fabric can enhance rich texture or color in the art.

Some framing and art supply stores stock fabric-covered mat board in a limited range of colors. Or you can purchase fabric and cover your mat yourself. There are advantages to both options.

The fabric-covered board is usually covered with high-quality linen or silk which might be difficult to find in local fabric stores. The surface is uniform and the cloth is well-mounted, with the grain running in a straight line parallel to the edge of the board. It also saves you a lot of time to buy the mat already covered with fabric. However, when you cut the window the bevel of the mat will be cardboard and the fabric may fray at the window's edge.

If you cover your own mat, you will be able to shop around for fabric and find exactly the color, pattern, and texture you want for a particular picture. Both the front of the mat and the bevel will be fabric-covered. Covering a mat with fabric isn't hard, just exacting, and it will add a personalized, hand-crafted touch to the framed piece.

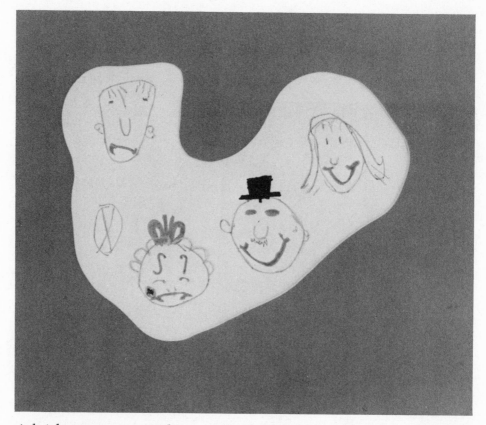

A bright green mat with an oddly shaped curved opening matches the playful mood of the drawing by Rachel Chessman.

PAINTED MAT BEVELS An easy way to liven up a mat is to paint the bevel. This is especially effective when you want to put a white mat on a picture with a white background but you want a touch of color to accent the picture.

Painting the bevel isn't hard; it's just tedious and it may take a little practice to get the feel of it. It is best to use a rag board mat because it takes the color better and mistakes can be shaved off.

FRENCH MATS French mats are a very old and charming tradition of decorative matting. You can see them often in art museums on very old etchings or drawings. Each mat is designed specifically for a particular piece of artwork, so each one will be different, but generally a French mat will have several lines around the window, one or more bands of pale color, and occasionally a band of gold leaf.

Sometimes the French mats you see in museums are the original

A color photograph is framed under glass with a fabric covered mat and a simple wood frame.

The white mat needs the contrasting bevel to delineate the edges of the three crayon paintings on white paper. The paintings are framed with rag board mat and backing, glass, and a metal-leafed wood frame.

41

A reproduction of an old etching depicting Grein, on the River Danube, is appropriately framed with a French mat painted in very pale blues and greens. The mat is rag board, and the frame is a carved wood one purchased at a flea market and refinished.

ones painted by the artist or one of his contemporaries. Other French mats have been cut and painted by an art lover or conservationist at a later date. In either case the colors will be very pale so as not to overpower the faded colors in an old piece of art.

You may own artwork which would be perfectly displayed in a traditional French mat, or you may want to use the idea of a French mat as a jumping-off place for designing decorative mats for more recent art. The possibilities are endless. The photograph shows a patterned band drawn with pen and ink around the window. A couple of bold lines, perhaps combined with a painted bevel, could look great (and still be proper enough) for a diploma or certificate. I have even seen a fabric-covered version with appliquéd lines around the window of a mat for a bright little piece of needlepoint.

Instructions for painting a traditional French mat appear in Chapter 11.

The mat for this imaginative drawing is decorated with a band of whimsical figures by the artist, Billy McDonald.

A close-up view of the same mat.

DOUBLE MATS A simple variation on the regular mat is the double mat, actually two mats for the same picture. The window of the top mat is larger than the window of the bottom mat, so a strip of the bottom mat is visible immediately around the picture. The mats can be measured so that the visible part of the bottom one is as narrow as ¹⁄₁₆" or as wide as desired. It is usually most effective if the two mats are different widths and both are a different width from the frame. If any widths are the same the repetition is usually distracting.

FLOATING ARTWORK ON MAT BOARD Instead of cutting a window in a piece of mat board, you may attach the art to the top surface of the board. The mat board showing around the sides of the artwork will give somewhat the same effect as a mat with a window cut out. This is a good method of matting something with uneven edges that would look awkward in a square mat or something with interesting edges that you don't want covered by the edge of a mat.

However, it is not archivally safe to frame such a piece in contact with glass. A solution is to float the art on the mat board and then cut

44

A nature watercolor by Marita Sandstrom is double matted with a thin band of orange around the picture and framed with a simple wood frame with a thin gold liner.

45

A small reproduction is dry mounted on a light-colored mat board and then matted with a dark mat. The silk-screen by Hundertwasser, is 690 Green Power © 1976 by Gruener Janura AG, Glarus, Switzerland.

another mat with a window large enough so that the edges of the artwork and part of the mat board behind it show.

You can dry mount or wet mount the artwork to the backing or stick it with Positionable Mounting Adhesive, but none of these methods is archival, so if you are concerned about preserving the artwork, hinge it to the backing with linen tape or acid-free rice paper and archival paste (Chapter 14).

7 Framing Suggestions

DIFFERENT KINDS OF ART, for aesthetic or practical reasons, require different kinds of frames. In this chapter you will find framing suggestions for categories of artwork that take into consideration the peculiar properties of each.

SILK-SCREEN PRINTS, ETCHINGS, AND LITHO-GRAPHS Original graphic art should be framed with a mat and glass for archival reasons. The mat is also necessary because oils in the ink will transfer a ghost image of the print onto the glass if the two are in contact. In any case, these prints usually look best with a mat.

Graphic art should be matted with the entire image, the artist's signature, and the plate mark, if there is one, visible through the window of the mat. The outside dimensions of the mat should be at least a little larger than the paper. Original graphic art is devalued by trimming, but if the mat absolutely must be smaller, the paper can be folded near the edge.

WATERCOLORS Watercolors should always be protected by a mat since they can be ruined easily by waterspotting if they are in contact with the glass.

Because of the nature of the medium, watercolors tend to warp and buckle. This is a natural tendency and should not be regarded as bad or inferior. Mounting a watercolor on a rigid backing not only reduces its value, but also obscures the natural characteristics of the paper.

PASTELS AND CHARCOAL AND PENCIL DRAWINGS
These should be matted, not only to protect them from moisture, but also because they smear easily and might be damaged by contact with the glass.

Acrylic should not be used with pastels, because the electric

47

An original serigraph print by Nikki Schuman is framed under glass with an antiqued metal-leafed frame and a rag mat.

charge built up by cleaning or brushing the acrylic can lift the tiny particles of pastel, even when it is separated from the acrylic by a mat.

RUBBINGS   Choosing mats and frames for rubbings is often difficult because rubbings are usually all one color. A mat of the same color is usually too strong and a black or white one is often too stark. Double mats can be effective — the band of color of the lower mat is usually just enough to accent a color in the rubbing. Fabric-covered

48

An oriental rubbing framed with a double mat. The frame was taken off of another picture and painted with a high-gloss enamel.

mats are often used on rubbings because ordinary mats appear flat next to the textured surface of the artwork.

Rubbings on thin paper wrinkle easily. Handmade rice paper, on which many Oriental rubbings are made, usually does not lie flat to begin with, and the process of rubbing introduces new stresses into the paper and often causes wrinkles and small tears. Wrinkles will straighten out to some extent as the paper hangs in the frame, but the rubbing will never lie absolutely flat unless mounted to a backing. I do not recommend mounting rubbings. The embossed quality is de-

49

stroyed and the natural characteristics of the paper — heavy or light-weight, porous or textured — are obscured. If a rubbing is still to look like a rubbing on paper it should not be mounted.

DIPLOMAS, CERTIFICATES, AND OTHER OFFICIAL PIECES OF PAPER Contrary to popular practice, diplomas and other documents should be matted and backed with 100 percent rag board for all the reasons discussed in Chapter 2. If you want it to be around for a long time, treat it well. And as long as you are putting a frame and mat on it, why not use a little ingenuity and do something interesting — a certificate can be proper without being somber. Try painting the bevel of the mat or adding a few thin lines around the window. Consider a natural wood molding with an oiled or stained finish or a metal frame, or shop at antique or secondhand stores for an old oak or maple frame.

PHOTOGRAPHS A photograph is a bit different from other art-work on paper because the top surface is coated with an emulsion that is extremely sensitive to scratches and fingerprints. If the photo-graph is framed against a piece of glass this emulsion can also host a mold growth that will cause the photograph to adhere to the glass. Once this happens the photograph is ruined, so photographs should be matted.

Unevenness is especially noticeable in glossy or very detailed photographs. The common solution to this problem is to dry mount the photo to a mat board or Fome-Cor backing. Dry mounting is the only way to get a photograph to lie absolutely flat in the frame. However, any original piece of artwork, including a photograph, will decrease in value if you mount it. Photographs can be flattened in a heat press — unless they are on resin-coated paper, in which case they will curl up when heated — or by pressing under a heavy stack of books for a few days. (You can identify resin-coated paper by the "plastic" feel of both the front and back surfaces.) Once you have flattened a photograph, the mat and glass will hold it as flat as any other artwork on paper.

If the photograph you have is not a valuable one, then dry mount-ing can be an effective solution. Several snapshots can be dry mounted collage fashion on one piece of board, or a photograph may be mounted on a backing and then matted.

A particularly striking presentation for some photographs is to cut a piece of particle board (a compressed sawdust board available at lumberyards) the same size as the photograph. Sand the edges and

A photograph by Frank Brevoort is matted and backed with rag board and framed under glass in a natural mahogany molding.

paint them with gesso to fill any crevices. When the gesso dries, sand the edges again lightly and then paint them black. Mount the photograph on the front with Positionable Mounting Adhesive.

The surface of a photograph may be dusted with a Photographer's Wipe, a lint-free cloth available at photography stores. If you spill liquid on the surface of the photograph, the emulsion will bubble. The only thing to do in this case is to rewash the photograph. Place it in clean running water for 10 or 15 minutes. Let it dry face-up on a paper towel or piece of blotting paper until the front surface is dry. Then turn it face-down (so that it will curl less) until it is completely dry — about 4 hours.

Black and white photographs are commonly framed with very wide white or off-white mats and simple frames of metal or of natural wood painted black. However, colored mats can also be effective with black and white photographs, and you will find that your color choice is not necessarily dictated by the grays in the photograph but by the mood of the picture.

Because a color photograph is full of slight color modulations, it is often nearly impossible to find a mat color that matches some color in the photo. The mats often look too flat or too harsh. The best solution often turns out to be a white or off-white mat or a double mat, since a thin line of color accents a similar color in the picture without overpowering it.

ACRYLIC AND OIL PAINTINGS Paintings are susceptible to damage from acid in the framing materials as well as abrasion, humidity, and dirt, so if you have a painting you would like to preserve, read the section in Chapter 2 about conservation of paintings and follow the necessary steps.

A canvas on a stretcher frame will have a depth of ⅝" or more. You will find that the easiest method of framing, which also looks best, is to use a frame that is as deep as or deeper than the stretcher.

Frames for paintings vary as widely as the styles of painting. Generally, wood frames with or without liners are used for traditional paintings. Modern paintings may look best with wood or metal strip-

A printed African fabric has been stretched on a wood stretcher frame and then framed with a simple wood molding.

ping, a standard wood frame, a metal frame, a floater frame, or no frame at all.

Acrylic and oil paintings are usually not framed with glass since they already have a protective coating.

If anything is allowed to lean against a painting on canvas, the canvas will stretch, resulting in a visible bulge. This is not something you can correct by yourself; consult an art conservator for help.

FABRIC AND NEEDLEWORK Most fabric and needlework pieces need to be stretched on a rigid backing before framing, but stiff pieces may be framed just like paper artwork, with glass and backing and a mat if you want one. Sometimes regular mat board looks stark next to the textured cloth, so you may want to use a fabric-covered mat. Fragments of old cloth or needlework, or pieces with interesting edges, may be sewn into place on a cloth-covered backing.

The most debated point about framing needlework is whether or not to put glass over it. Glass will keep it from getting dirty but it can also obscure the texture and richness of the needlework. Most people

A wood dowel sewn to the back along the top edge supports this Navajo weaving.

who frame needlework feel very strongly one way or the other and either stand is valid. Scotchgard and other protective fabric sprays are commonly used to protect fabric when glass is not desirable. These sprays repel water and dirt and make the surface of the cloth easier to clean but they may also change the appearance of the fabric.

Any piece that is very old and fragile or very valuable should not be sprayed but should be framed under glass instead.

TAPESTRIES, WEAVINGS, AND RUGS Hang textiles by attaching a wood or metal strip to the top edge. There are three acceptable ways to do this. You can sew a wood or aluminum rod or slat to the back of the fabric at the top edge with heavy-duty thread or nylon fishing line. This method is not satisfactory for heavy items, however, since they tend to sag between the stitches. To distribute the weight of the textile more evenly, cut a narrow strip of linen or muslin as long as the textile is wide and fold it in half to form a pocket which you can then sew to the back of the fabric near the top edge. Slip the wood or metal piece through this pocket.

Velcro can also be used to hang light or heavy textiles. Sew the "female" strip to the back of the textile along the top edge, and staple the "male" strip to a wood slat which you can then hang on the wall.

MOSAICS AND STAINED GLASS The two major problems with mosaics and stained-glass compositions are that they are very heavy and they are very often out of square.

Be sure to choose a frame that is hefty enough to support the weight of the piece. When you are choosing a molding, look at the width of the back edge. This should be at least ¾" for pieces up to 16"

A strong wood frame is necessary to support the weight of this stained glass composition by Debby Lamden.

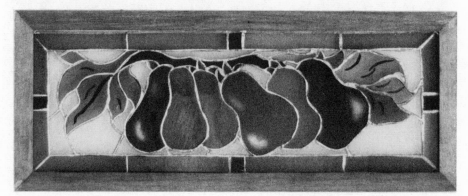

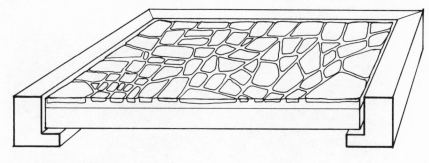

A frame with the molding reversed

x 20″, and at least 1″ for larger frames. Use extra screw eyes when you attach the wire for hanging or use strap hangers.

Since stained-glass pieces are often hung in windows where both sides may be viewed, you may want to fasten the picture into the frame with thin wood strips and finish the back of the frame according to the instructions for double-sided frames.

Mosaics are sometimes framed as trays or tabletops. A good way to do this is to turn a wooden molding upside-down so that the lip supports the mosaic from underneath and the inside edge of the frame fits flush against the side of the mosaic. What is normally the back edge of the frame becomes the front, or top edge in this case, so you will have to finish the back edge of the molding.

THREE-DIMENSIONAL OBJECTS The first decision to make when framing something three-dimensional is whether or not to put glass over it. Anything that might be ruined by dust or moisture, or anything valuable, old, or fragile, should be framed behind glass. Other objects, such as wooden masks, sand castings, or relief carvings, either do not need the protection of glass or would lose their textural quality.

Some items are rigid enough that they don't need any additional support, but most three-dimensional artwork must be attached to a stiff backing. This backing should be sturdy enough to support the weight of the artwork without warping, but not so heavy that it can't be hung safely. The object should be mounted in such a way that it will not be damaged if you need to remove it later.

If you are framing with glass, there must be a space between the glass and the backing wide enough to accommodate the object. To accomplish this you must use a deep frame and put spacers behind the glass to separate it from the backing.

If the piece is particularly heavy, you must choose a molding

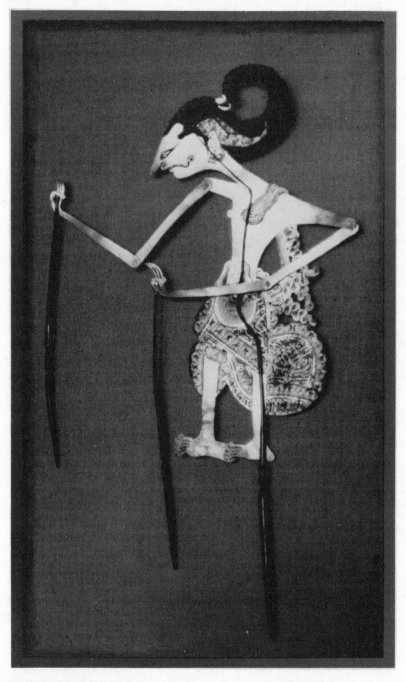

56 *The backing in this frame is plywood, covered with a bright orange fabric. Tiny tacks secure the puppet to wood dowels that extend about ¼" above the surface of the backing.*

with a large enough cross section to support the weight of the piece and use extra hardware to hang it.

OVERSIZED PICTURES   If your artwork is larger than 30″ x 40″ it may take longer to find the materials you need.

Standard matboard size is 32″ x 40″. Oversized mat board, 40″ x 60″, is available at some art supply stores and frame stores but only in a limited range of colors. One solution is to cut half a mat from one sheet of mat board and the other half from a second sheet, join the two halves with tape, and then cover the whole thing with fabric so that the seam won't show. Or you can look for a store that stocks and cuts mat board the size you need. Many frame stores don't have equipment large enough to machine-cut a window in an oversized mat board, so call before you go.

For glass larger than 30″ x 40″, you may have to go to a glass company. In large sizes, purchase double-weight glass: it is less likely to break. And have the glass cut to the size you need; large-sized glass is dangerous and expensive, so you don't want to risk breaking it. I recommend using acrylic, which is lightweight and doesn't break, for very large pictures. However, it is not satisfactory in some large clip frames, where it tends to bend.

The best backing for a large picture is Fome-Cor, which is fairly stiff, lightweight, and available in large sizes. Two pieces of corrugated cardboard can also form a good stiff backing if one is cut with the corrugations vertical and the other with the corrugations horizontal.

An oversized picture will be heavy (especially if you are using glass) so choose a frame that will be strong enough to support the picture. The molding should be at least 1″ across on the back edge. Use heavy-duty hanging techniques as described in Chapter 33.

Materials and Skills

2

8 Framing Tools and Materials

YOU DON'T NEED big or fancy tools for framing. In fact, many of the tools you need, you may already have. The following is a general list of framing tools. Depending on the types of frames you build, you may or may not use all of them. The tools and materials in this list can be purchased at a hardware store unless otherwise stated.

RULER OR TAPE MEASURE You can measure artwork and framing materials with either a ruler or a tape measure. It's easier to hold everything flat with a ruler and it's easier to line up the end exactly with the end of the artwork. The metal piece on the very end of the tape measure obscures the first several lines and can be a hindrance when you are trying to measure something accurately, but there will probably be times when you need to measure something that is longer than your ruler, so a tape measure will come in handy as well. If you buy a metal ruler or one with a metal edge, you can also use it for a straightedge. Whichever you buy, make sure it is marked off in sixteenths.

METAL STRAIGHTEDGE You will need a metal straightedge for cutting straight lines with the mat knife. Wood or plastic won't do, because the knife can cut right into the edge, ruining both the straightedge and the artwork. A wood ruler with a metal strip on the edge is fine. Metal rulers are available in several lengths, plain or with a no-slip cork or rubber backing. The no-slip backing is *definitely* worth the higher price, for it will save you hours of frustration from crooked cuts; it is also harder to find. An alternative is to put masking tape or felt on the back of a plain metal ruler. It will be easiest for you if you purchase a straightedge as long as most of the items you will be framing. Metal straightedges with and without numbered graduations are sold at art supply and office supply stores.

MITER BOX A very simple hardwood miter box costs $2 to $5. A

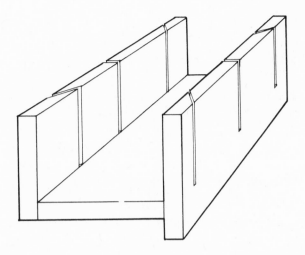

metal one with a saw held in place and an angle gauge can run as high as $25 or $30. It takes some practice to cut a perfect miter with any miter box. If you are using a very simple one, the saw can easily wobble or tilt slightly, resulting in a crooked cut, but you will probably find that with some practice you can cut a perfectly good corner with a simple miter box. I am perfectly happy with mine, which is of hardwood and is the simplest and cheapest available. But if you plan to cut a lot of frames, you may decide to invest in the metal one.

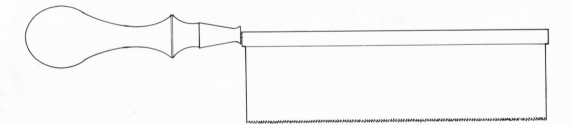

BACKSAW A fine-toothed backsaw, with a stiff rib running along the top, is commonly used with a miter box. The more teeth per inch, the smoother your cut will be: buy one with 12 or 16 points to the inch. Backsaws cost $3 to $8.

HACKSAW A hacksaw is a very fine-toothed saw with a thin blade, used for cutting metal. A small one costs $2 to $5.

VISE OR CORNER CLAMP Simple corner clamps cost about $4 and are perfectly satisfactory for almost any frame. They screw onto a wood board or work bench. Some corner clamps have an extra piece that holds a saw in position to cut a mitered corner, eliminating the need for a miter box; these are only slightly more expensive than the regular corner clamp. You will also see large corner vises costing $15 and up when you shop for corner clamps. These are not necessary unless you are working with very wide moldings. When you buy a corner clamp, check to see what the limitations are. Most can't take a molding over 3″ or 4″ wide and can't join a frame less than 3″ on a side.

GLUE   The corner of a picture frame is a very weak joint because end grains are joined, so a very strong glue is essential. Titebond, an aliphatic resin glue that is commonly used by framers and other wood craftsmen, is the one I recommend.

BRADS   Wire brads are used instead of nails for framing. They are thin and have almost no heads. Purchase brads as long as your molding is wide, and buy the thinnest ones you can find — 16 gauge to 22 gauge.

HAND DRILL   A simple hand drill costs from $4 to $10. It is not necessary to purchase drill bits since most moldings are soft enough so that you can drill with one of the same brads you plan to use in the frame.

PLIERS   A small pair of needlenose pliers with a wire cutter is the kind you want.

HAMMER   A very lightweight tack hammer is sufficient. Some people prefer hammers with resin heads — they don't dent the molding as easily as metal hammers. You can purchase a simple tack hammer for as little as $1, but one with a resin head will cost more.

NAIL SET   A nail set is a tool with a pointed end used to tap nails in until they're just below the surface of the wood. Purchase the one with the smallest point you can find. ⅟₃₂″ is preferable.

FITTING TOOL   Used for pushing brads into the back of the frame to hold everything in place, this is a tool made specifically for the framing trade and it is hard to get retail. You may order one from Twin City Moulding and Supply for about $12.

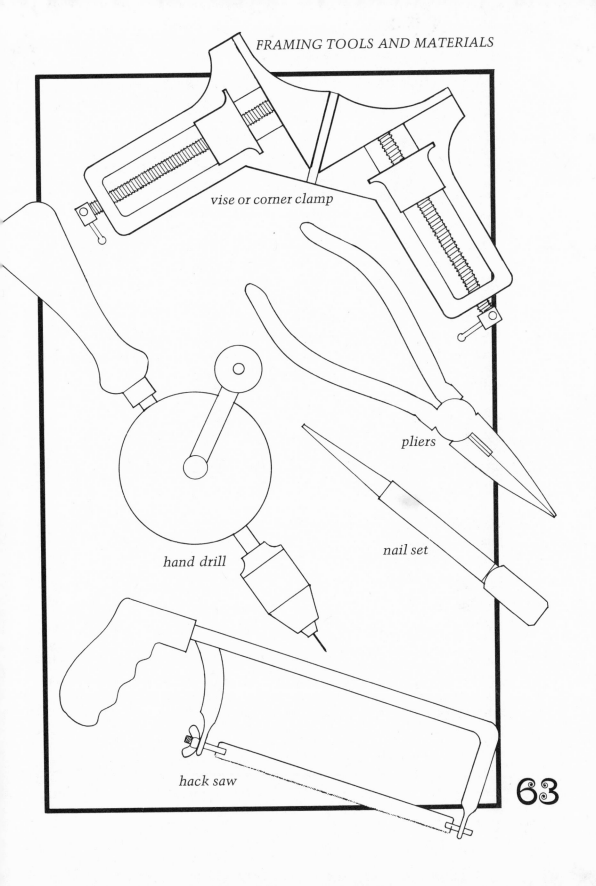

vise or corner clamp

pliers

hand drill

nail set

hack saw

AWL An awl is a pointed tool used for starting holes for screws or screw eyes. It usually costs less than $1, but you can also substitute a small nail.

MAT KNIFE Buy the kind with the flat chunky handle (not the kind with the long skinny handle) because it is safer and easier to control. The ones with retractable blades will be safer to keep around the house. These are available at art supply and hobby stores as well as hardware stores. They cost around $2.

STAPLE GUN Used for stapling canvas or fabric on a backing. You don't need a super-heavy-duty one, but you need something more than a desk stapler. A small staple gun will cost $6 to $10.

CLAMPS You will need clamps for holding wood or metal pieces in the miter box while you are cutting them. C-clamps come in several sizes and have a screw-type adjustment. They cost $1 to $3. Spring clamps are simpler and cost a little less, but they can be used only for small moldings.

GLASS CUTTER A glass cutter is a small sharp wheel set into a metal handle. It is used for scoring glass, and costs about $1.

PLASTIC CUTTER A plastic cutter has a sharp blade for scoring acrylic. It also costs about $1.

RULING PEN A ruling pen is used for drawing lines on French mats. The ink is held between two metal points which are adjustable for different line widths.

LINEN TAPE Also called Holland Tape, this is an archival tape used for attaching artwork to a mat or backing. It can be purchased from a bookbinding supplier or a framing supplier. You can order it from Talas or Twin City Moulding and Supply. A roll 1" wide by 150

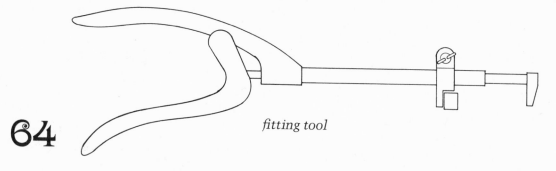

fitting tool

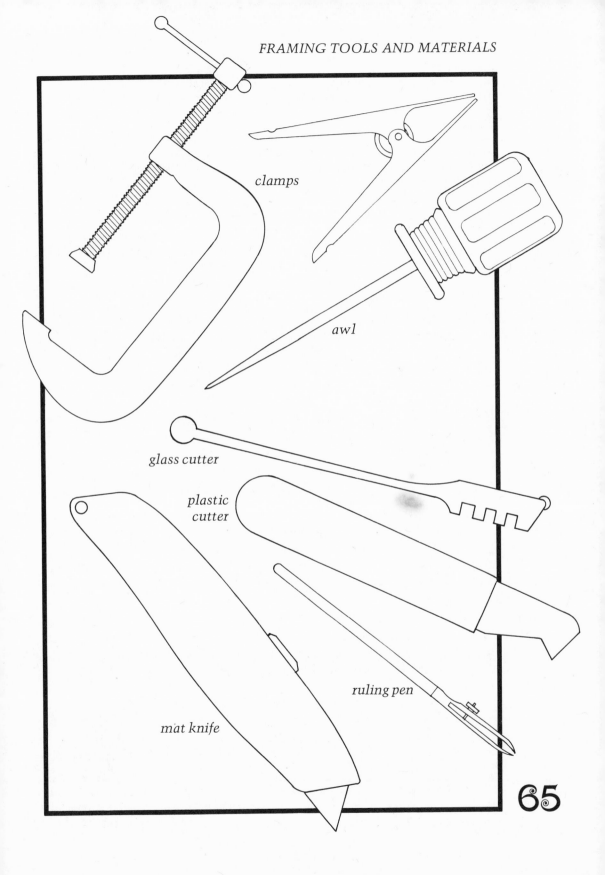

clamps

awl

glass cutter

plastic
cutter

ruling pen

mat knife

65

yards long costs about $9. You may be able to buy it in small quantities from a local frame shop.

ACID-FREE RICE PAPER HINGES Rice paper hinges and archival paste are an alternative to linen tape. Acid-free rice paper is hard to find. You may find it in some art supply stores or you can order it from Talas.

ARCHIVAL PASTE An acid-free paste for mounting artwork with rice paper hinges. You can use a methyl cellulose paste available from Talas or Twin City Moulding and Supply, or you can make your own rice paste following the recipe on page 114.

MUSEUM MOUNTING KIT Another alternative to linen tape. The kit contains acid-free hinges and archival paste for mounting artwork to a mat or backing. You can order it from Talas.

PRITT GLUE STICK A non-messy method of mounting artwork. The glue stick is not acidic. Buy it at an art supply store.

DOUBLE STICK TAPE Used for sticking double mats together or sticking mats to backings. Sold in dime stores.

ARCHIVIST'S PEN A pen to test the acidity of paper and mat board. It can be ordered from Talas and costs about $5.

WORK SURFACE When you are finishing a molding or building a frame, you will be working with messy materials — glue, putty, paint, or varnish — which could easily ruin a mat or a piece of artwork. Spread paper over your work area so you can clean up easily, and keep artwork and mat board somewhere else until the messy jobs are done.

When you are working with artwork or mats, a clean sheet of paper is a suitable work surface. Keep an old sheet or other soft cloth handy to spread over the table when you are working with a metal frame or a finished wood molding that scratches easily.

CUTTING SURFACE Whenever you cut mats or backings you will cut into the surface underneath, so set aside a piece of chipboard or Upson board (or any cheap cardboard) to use as a cutting surface. A harder surface such as plywood or masonite is less satisfactory because it will dull the blade more quickly. Use a fresh cutting surface when you cut mat windows since scores in the cutting surface can result in a ragged cut. Keep the cutting surface free of glue or putty.

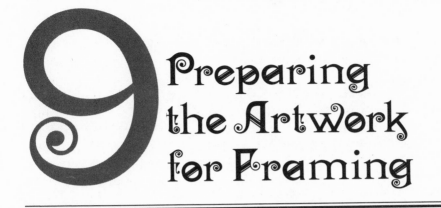

Preparing the Artwork for Framing

THIS CHAPTER COVERS all the little things that you may need to do to your artwork before you can measure it or frame it. Little things, but important ones, since it is easy to ruin the work if you don't do them correctly.

REMOVING ARTWORK FROM A FRAME From time to time you will need to remove art from a frame either to put it in a new frame, to replace an old mat or a broken piece of glass, or to reaffix a picture that has fallen down inside the frame. The primary concern here is that you do not injure the artwork. Usually you will not know who framed the artwork or how it was done, so it is best not to take any chances.

Place the frame face-down on a clean cloth or sheet of paper.

Remove the screw eyes and wire from the frame completely so that they can't scratch the artwork.

In most cases the frame will have a sheet of brown paper glued over the back of it. There should be a stiff backing of some kind (cardboard, Fome-Cor, or even wood) between the brown paper seal and the art, but don't count on it. Lift the corner of the brown paper and peek underneath. If there is indeed a backing then you may take your mat knife or razor blade and cut an X from corner to opposite corner and peel the brown paper from the frame. If there is no backing behind the art, do not use a knife to slit the paper, but peel it from the back of the frame, being careful not to injure the art.

Use needlenose pliers to remove any brads or diamond-shaped points which hold the backing in place.

Reach under the frame and press along one edge of the glass to lift it out of the frame. Remove all the contents of the frame together. If the glass is broken, do not reach under the frame; instead, pry the backing out of the frame and carefully lift out the contents, one piece at a time. Do not press on the back of the frame or allow the artwork to slide around in the frame, for the edges of broken glass can easily damage the art.

REMOVING THE ART FROM A MAT OR BACKING

Paper artwork is usually attached to a mat or backing with tape or paper hinges. It should be attached only at the top and the tape should be acid-free (which means it won't stain the artwork) with a water-soluble adhesive, but don't depend on it. It is common to open the back of a frame and find that a previous framer has attached the artwork firmly on all four sides with masking tape, or glued it to the backing with rubber cement, or mounted it so tightly to the backing that it can't be removed.

If the artwork is attached with tape, the first thing to try is peeling the tape off — gently. Always peel away from the artwork. (If you peel the tape toward the artwork you are more likely to tear the paper.) If linen tape or rice paper hinges don't readily peel off, they can usually be removed with a little water: moisten a cotton swab with water and daub it on the tape. Proceed to lift the hinge and daub the underside to further dissolve the glue. If water doesn't work, try saliva. And if all of these methods fail, use a sharp mat knife to slice the hinge even with the edge of the paper.

Note: Don't use water if you are likely to dampen any painted or inked area of the artwork. The colors are likely to be water-soluble, so it is better to cut the hinge with a mat knife.

If you need help removing masking tape or glue from the back of a piece of valuable art, consult a professional conservator.

CLEANING THE ARTWORK

Smudges can be removed with an eraser. I recommend using an Artgum eraser, which is stiff, rectangular, and yellowish, or a kneaded eraser, which is gray and pliable, or a Magic Rub eraser, a plastic compound which is safer than rubber and contains no grit.

If you have a painting or artwork on paper that needs an overall cleaning, consult a professional conservator.

FLATTENING ARTWORK ON PAPER

Posters that have been rolled up can be flattened in a dry mount press. This is not a satisfactory method for original artwork because heat may affect the ink or paint, and any embossed areas would be flattened.

Original or valuable items, except for photographs, should be flattened as follows:

Place the work face-down on a sheet of blotting paper.

Spray the piece from a few feet away with a fine mist of water.

You don't want to make the art wet. Just barely moisten it until you see the paper relax. Then place another piece of blotter paper on top of the artwork. Place a piece of glass or plywood on top to weight it, and allow it to dry for several hours.

TRIMMING AND FOLDING ARTWORK Original artwork should never be trimmed. People do take seriously the artist's conception of the image in relation to the entire sheet of paper, and therefore artwork is devalued by trimming.

Artwork that is not original or valuable can be trimmed as follows:

Place the piece face-up on a clean cutting surface.

Arrange clean napkins or tissues on the face of the artwork so the straightedge won't scratch it.

Draw a very light pencil line where you want to trim.

Place a metal straightedge over the artwork with one edge along the cutting line. Make sure you have a sharp blade in the mat knife.

Hold the straightedge firmly in place and cut slowly.

Trimming the artwork with a mat knife and a metal straightedge. Sarsaparilla © Portal Publications, Sausalito, Cal.

69

10 Measuring

THE FOLLOWING ARE general guidelines for measuring artwork for framing and for measuring the framing materials before cutting them.

Never assume that the artwork is rectangular. You can check this easily by measuring across the two diagonals; if the measurements are the same, the corners are square.

Always take two or three measurements in each direction when you are measuring artwork. Measure across the center and at each end. This way, if there are discrepancies you will catch them This is especially important for stretched fabric that is bulky at the corners.

Measure accurately to a sixteenth of an inch.

Check and double-check your measurements. It's better to take a long time measuring than to cut a valuable material the wrong size.

Hold paper artwork flat and stretch fabric to its full width when you measure it.

Anything to be mounted and then framed should be measured for the frame *after* mounting and trimming. Mounted paper is flatter

Measure the two diagonals to find out if the corners are square.
Take several measurements in each direction.

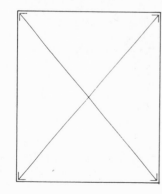 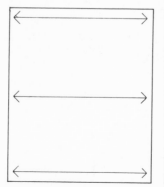 

and easier to measure accurately, and after it is mounted and trimmed the piece may be slightly larger or smaller than you anticipated.

Whenever you are marking cutting lines on mats, backings, or the artwork itself, use pencil instead of ink — ink can smear or run and damage the artwork.

To avoid confusion, always note the width first and the height second when you write down measurements.

When you measure, remember to include the necessary tolerances:

A wooden frame must be ⅛" larger than the mat, glass, artwork, or backing.

A mat must overlap the edge of the paper at least ⅛" on every side to keep the artwork in place.

Stretching fabric around a backing or stretcher bar will add ¹⁄₁₆" to ¼" to the measurement of the backing by itself. Stretch it on the backing and then measure it for the frame.

When measuring an already assembled frame for mat, glass, or backing, turn the frame face-down on the table and measure the opening at the back of the frame. Then subtract ⅛" from each measurement for the exact size of the contents. Old frames are often loose at the corners. They should be repaired before measuring. They may also be warped, so take several measurements in each direction.

Measure the opening at the back of the frame.

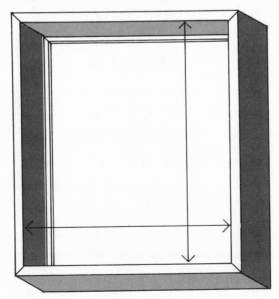

11 Mats

A MAT SERVES two purposes in a frame. It provides a space between the glass and the artwork, greatly reducing the possibility that water-spotting or mold growth might damage the art. It also provides a visual separation, a neutral zone, between the artwork and the frame.

If a mat does not look right with the piece you are framing and you don't want the glass resting on the artwork, you can insert spacers between artwork and glass when you fasten everything into the frame (Chapter 21).

PURCHASING MAT BOARD You can buy mat board at frame shops and art supply stores. It comes in sheets 32" x 40", and some stores also stock sheets 40" x 60" in a limited selection of colors.

Mat board comes in three thicknesses, two-, four-, and eight-ply. Four-ply is the standard size stocked in framing and art supply stores. It is 1/16" thick and is recommended for general use. Two-ply is very thin, about 1/32". It can be used whenever a four-ply mat board is too thick, but remember that the purpose of the mat is to lift the glass off the artwork: when you want to use a two-ply mat, make sure your artwork does not have raised areas that might come in contact with the glass. Two-ply *rag* board is commonly used as an acid-free backing in front of the stiff backing in the frame, and for mounting and matting photographs.

Eight-ply mat board, also called double-weight, is about 1/8" thick and is sometimes used for the special effect of the wider bevel, when extra stiffness is needed, or when there are raised areas of the artwork that would touch the glass if a four-ply mat board were used.

Wood pulp mat board, just like any other wood pulp product, contains acid which will eventually deteriorate the artwork. The surface of the mat board is close to neutral pH, but the inside is acidic and the acid fumes breathe onto the artwork from the cut edge of the mat. This causes the artwork to turn brown and brittle over a period of years. One hundred percent rag board is made from cloth rather than wood pulp and is chemically neutral or very close to neutral. (To test the pH of your rag board, you can order an archivist's pen from Talas.) An acid-free rag board will not damage your art (provided the work itself is on high quality paper — paper that is very acidic will become brittle and yellow anyway).

Museums use only 100 percent rag board, hence its other name, museum board. Rag board comes only in a few shades of white and off-white, but if you want to have a colored mat and still have the protection of rag board, there is an alternative. Buy a sheet of good quality colored paper and dry mount it to one surface of a sheet of rag board (Chapter 15). I recommend using Color-Aid, Pantone, or Canson paper, available from art supply stores. The bevel of the mat will still be the color of the rag board, so be sure to choose a shade that is compatible with the artwork.

A new product, not widely available, is an acid-free wood pulp mat board called conservation mounting board. It is chemically neutral, it comes in the same range of colors as rag board, and it costs less than 100 percent rag board.

Rag board is more than twice as expensive as wood pulp mat board. However, it holds up much longer, protects your artwork forever, and looks like the high-quality product that it is.

Whenever you purchase wood pulp board or rag board, check it for flaws in the surface, bent corners, or dents in the edge.

If you need to know whether a mat you already have is rag board look at the cut edge. Rag board will be the same color inside as on the surface; the center of a wood pulp board will be a different color from its surface. The texture of rag board is slightly rougher than the texture of wood pulp board, and rag board is heavier than other mat board.

MEASURING THE MAT

The Size of the Mat Opening The artwork you are matting may take up the entire sheet of paper or it may be placed in the center with a border of blank paper all around it. If the art covers the entire sheet, there are two ways to mat it. You can cut a mat window just a little smaller than the sheet of paper so that the inside edges of the mat overlap the paper about ⅛" on each side. Or you can cut the mat window larger than the paper so that the edges of the paper and some of the backing behind the artwork are visible. If you do this, you will want to choose a backing compatible with both the artwork and the mat.

It doesn't work to cut a mat window exactly the size of the paper — the paper will expand naturally and buckle when it hits the edge of the mat. It's difficult to measure and cut that precisely, and the artwork is likely to be out-of-square anyway, so it's likely to turn out looking like a mistake. If you want the edges of the paper to show, cut the mat window at least ½" larger than the paper in each direction. This will leave ¼" of backing showing all around the paper.

If the artwork is printed in the center of the paper with a border of blank paper all around, there are three ways you can mat it: You can cut the mat so that it covers the entire border and only the artwork is visible through the window. You can cut the window large enough so that the artwork and some of the border around it are visible. Or you can cut a window so large that the entire piece of paper and some of the backing behind it show through the opening.

In any of these situations, you have the option of cutting the window small enough to crop out part of the picture.

When framing original graphic art, it is customary to leave ¼" or more of the border showing at the top and sides of the print and enough border at the bottom to show the artist's signature. A print taken from a metal plate will have a plate mark, an embossed line around the picture. In this case you should leave ⅛" or more of the border showing around the plate mark. This convention allows the viewer to enjoy the entire image as the artist planned it and to see for himself, by the plate mark, the signature, and the layering of ink at the edge of the print, that the print is authentic.

To help you decide how large the window should be, use several pieces of white paper or scraps of mat board to block out an opening around the artwork.

Measuring the Artwork   Take two or three measurements in each direction — near each end and across the middle. If this sounds overly cautious, remember that commercial reproductions, the artist's paper, and printing plates are very often out of square.

The mat must extend ⅛" over the edge of the artwork on each side to hold it in place.

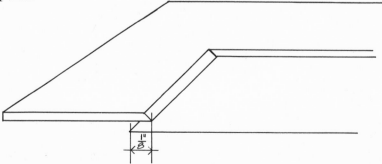

If the artwork covers the entire sheet of paper and you want the inside edges of the mat to barely cover the edges of the paper, measure the paper and subtract ¼". This allows the inside edge of the mat to overlap the edge of the paper ⅛" on each side and hold it in place.

If you want to cut a window large enough that the edges of the paper will show, measure the paper and add ½" or more, depending on how much of the backing you want showing.

If the artwork has a border around it and you want to cover the entire border with the mat, measure only the image and subtract ¼". This allows the inside edge of the mat to overlap the image by ⅛" on each side, leaving a slight margin for error when you cut the mat and guaranteeing that none of the border will show.

If you want to leave part of the border showing, measure the image and add the widths of the borders you want showing.

Draw a diagram of the mat and record the window measurements.

The Width of the Mat Margins   If possible, view a sample of the mat and a sample of the molding alongside the artwork while you are making this decision, as the width and color of the frame may help to determine the width of the mat.

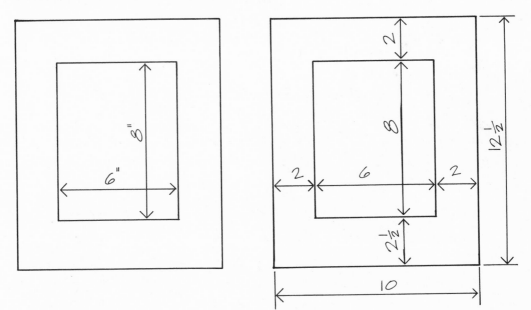

It is usual to make the bottom margin of the mat a little larger than the top and sides. This compensates for an optical illusion — if the mat is the same size all around, the bottom will look smaller because the picture appears to be sitting closer to the bottom of the frame than it actually is. If the mat is slightly larger on the bottom it will look the same size on all four sides. To adjust for the optical illusion, make the bottom of the mat ¼" larger if the top and sides are less than 2½", ½" larger if the top and sides are between 2½" and 4", and 1" larger if the top and sides are more than 4".

Some people prefer to make the mat noticeably larger on the bottom than on the top and sides. If you want this look, be sure to compensate for the optical illusion and then add to the bottom dimension.

Note the sizes of the mat margins on your diagram.

Finding the Outer Dimension of the Mat   Add the horizontal dimensions of the mat window to the two side borders to get the overall horizontal dimension of the mat. Add the vertical dimension of the mat window to the top and bottom borders to get the overall vertical dimension of the mat. Note both dimensions on your diagram. Check and double-check both your measurements and your addition since this is not only the size for the mat, but also for the glass, backing, and frame.

CUTTING THE MAT
TOOLS
> *Metal straightedge*
> *Mat knife*
> *Dexter cutter (optional)*

To Cut the Perimeter of the Mat   Check the front surface of the mat board for flaws, bent corners, or dents along the edge. Mark the position of any flaws on the back of the board so that you can cut around them.

Place the mat board face-down on a clean cutting surface.

Start from one corner of the mat board. Measure to find the other two sides and mark them with a pencil and straightedge.

Double-check your measurements.

Cut along the lines you have just drawn using a metal straightedge and a mat knife. Make sure you have a sharp blade in the mat knife. Hold the ruler tightly, for it can easily slip. Draw the mat knife toward you along the straightedge, exerting only light pressure. On the first cut you only want to make a groove for the mat knife to follow on subsequent cuts. Proceed to cut through the mat using the metal straightedge as a guide and using as much pressure as is comfortable for you. Don't worry if you don't get through the mat in one or two cuts. Just keep cutting until you do cut through it.

To Cut the Mat Window   You can cut the window with either a mat knife or a Dexter Mat Cutter. (It is easier to get a uniform bevel with a Dexter cutter but many people find them hard to use.)

You can cut the mat window with a bevelled edge or a straight cut. The bevelled cut is more common and most people feel that it looks more professional. It is also harder to cut.

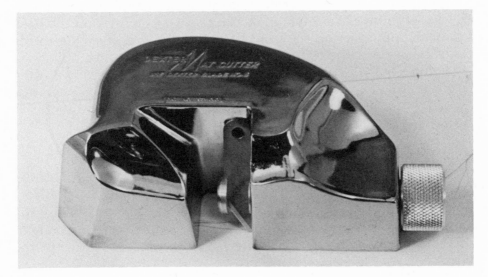

A Dexter Cutter.

Regardless of the tool you use or the kind of window you decide to cut, it takes practice to cut a mat window. Experiment on a piece of scrap mat board before you attempt to cut a real mat. If you have trouble, vary the amount of pressure you are using and the speed of cutting. Make sure your blade is sharp. They dull more quickly than you might think. Readjust the blade if you are using a Dexter cutter. Try to make the cut in one smooth motion; if you stop and start in the middle of a cut you are likely to get a bumpy cut.

Place the mat board *face-down* on the cutting surface with the bottom of the mat toward you. Place your sketch in front of you. Measure in from each edge to determine the position of the window. Mark the edges of the window opening with a straightedge and pencil. Then measure the window to double-check your measurements.

A STRAIGHT CUT WITH A MAT KNIFE   Place the metal straight- **77** edge along your pencil line. Hold it tightly and use it to guide the blade of the mat knife. Do not slant the mat knife to either side as this would result in a bevelled cut. Pull the mat knife toward you and start and stop your cuts exactly at the corners of the window.

A BEVELLED CUT WITH A MAT KNIFE   You can't use a straight-edge to make a bevelled cut, since the blade of the mat knife will slip right under the straightedge. Hold the mat knife at an angle with the handle slanted toward the center of the mat. At the end farthest from you insert the blade of the mat knife about ⅛" beyond the corner of the mat window. (You must overcut the corners a little on the back for the cuts to meet on the front.) Holding the mat steady with the other hand, draw the mat knife toward you. To do this, lock your wrist and elbow in position and pull the mat knife toward you using your whole body, not just your arm. You must go all the way through the mat board in one cut. Overcut at the bottom of the line about ⅛" also.

A BEVELLED CUT USING A DEXTER CUTTER   Adjust the blade in the cutter so that you have the slant you want and the blade extends the correct distance. To determine the position of the blade, place the Dexter cutter at one edge of the piece of mat board with the blade extending over the edge. It is adjusted properly when the tip of the blade just barely scratches the cutting surface underneath the mat board.

Cutting a mat window with a mat knife.

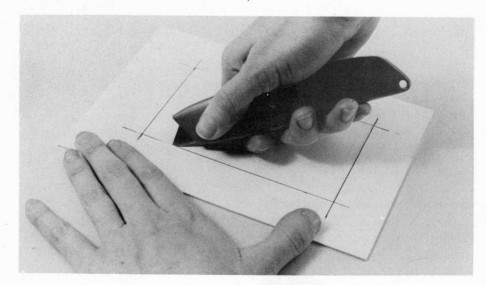

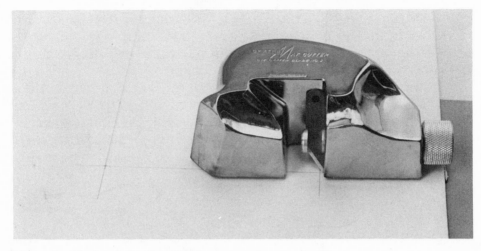

Place the blade of the Dexter Cutter on the cutting line.

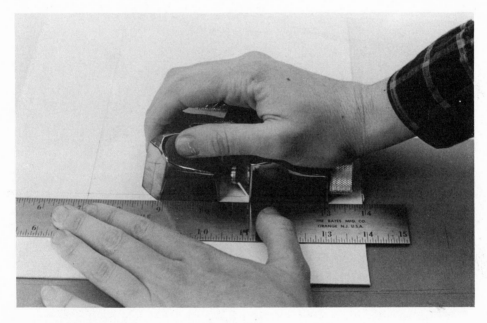

Cutting a mat window with a Dexter Cutter.

Place the Dexter cutter over the window of the mat. Set the blade into the mat board at the corner closest to you. If you are cutting a bevelled edge, start the cut about ⅛" beyond the corner. If you are making a straight cut, start the cut right on the corner of the window. Place the straightedge against the side of the cutter. Since the blade is set in from the side of the cutter, the straightedge will not be along the cutting line, but about ¼" away from it. Make sure the straightedge is parallel to the cutting line. Using the straightedge as a guide, push the Dexter cutter away from you. End the cut about ⅛" beyond the far corner if you are cutting a bevelled edge, at the corner if you are making a straight cut.

If the corners of the mat aren't cut all the way through cut them from the front with a sharp blade as shown. Then lightly sand any rough spots on the bevel with an emery board. Kneaded erasers are good for taking smudges off mats, and pastels are good for touching up nicks or scratches.

Cutting the corners of the mat window.

MULTIPLE-WINDOW MATS   I find that a good way to visualize the proportions of a mat with several windows is to place the pictures on a large piece of mat board the color you intend to use and move them until you establish the relationships you want. Use strips of mat board or paper to cover the edges of the mat so that you can determine the sizes of the mat margins. Usually the margins of the mat are wider than the spaces between the windows, and the bottom of the mat is a little wider than the top and side margins.

If your mat has only two or three windows, make a rough sketch of it. If it has several windows and it looks as though it will be rather confusing to measure, carefully place a sheet of tracing paper over the pictures and trace with a pencil (very lightly so that you don't injure the artwork) the outlines of all the windows. Remove the tracing paper, still without disturbing the position of the pictures. You now have a sketch that is to scale, so that if you forget to take a crucial measurement (and it is very easy to forget one when you are measuring many windows) you can just measure your sketch.

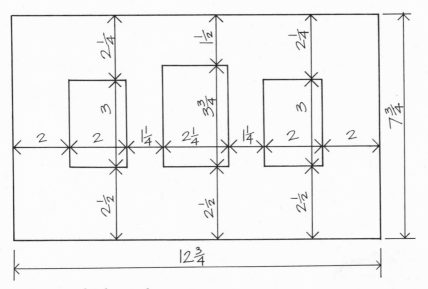

Measuring a multiple window mat.

At this point your sketch will show the windows as they look from the front of the mat. Since you will be laying out and cutting the windows from the back of the mat, you must reverse the sketch. So turn the tracing paper over and trace the drawing from the front of the paper onto the back. Now you are ready to measure.

Determine the size of each window by accurately measuring the artwork just as you would for a regular mat. Note the horizontal and vertical measurements for each window on your sketch.

Next measure the spaces between the pictures and record these measurements on your sketch. Remember when you take these measurements that the mat must overlap the artwork at least ⅛" on every side.

Measure and record the margins of the mat.

You need to have at least one string of dimensions running all the way across the sketch in each direction. Add the horizontal dimensions together to find the overall horizontal dimension. Add the vertical dimensions together to find the overall vertical measurement. Note the outside measurements of the mat on your sketch.

Cutting a Multiple-Window Mat Actual cutting is the same as noted above for a standard mat. Cut the outside perimeter of the mat first, then use your sketch to draw all the windows onto the back of the mat board. Double-check your measurements before cutting. Cut each window following the instructions for cutting a standard mat

81

A multiple window mat provides an interesting way to display the family pictures, even when they are different colors and sizes.

window. To insure that a bevelled cut is slanting the right way, the mat knife or Dexter cutter should always be over the window, not over the margin.

MATS WITH CURVED WINDOWS Occasionally you will need a mat with a circular, oval, or oddly shaped curved opening. What are commonly called oval mat openings are usually ellipses. Mats with circular and elliptical openings can be purchased in standard sizes. However, your artwork may not be a standard size, or you may not find the mat in the color you want, or you may just want to cut it yourself.

You can purchase a template for circles or ellipses at an architectural supply store or you can construct your own circle or ellipse with the following instructions:

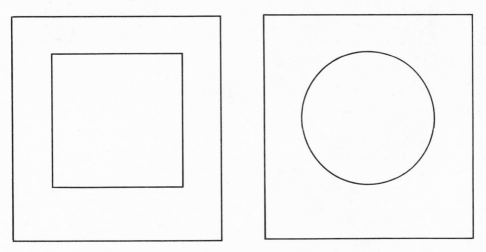

A three inch border around a circular opening looks larger than a three inch border around a rectangular opening.

The first step is to determine the size of the window: the diameter of a circle or the horizontal and vertical axes of an ellipse. Draw a diagram of the mat and note the size of the window opening. If your mat is to overlap the edge of the artwork, be sure to make the window ¼" smaller than the artwork in each direction.

Next decide how wide the margins of the mat should be. Note the measurement from the widest part of the window to the edge of the mat. Remember that a mat that measures 3" from the circular opening to the edge will look larger than a mat with a rectangular opening and a 3" border. Center the opening just above the center of the mat board, just as you do with a rectangular opening.

Add the horizontal window dimension to the two side margins to determine the overall horizontal dimension of the mat. Add the vertical window dimension to the top and bottom margins of the mat to find the overall vertical dimension.

Cut the perimeter of the mat board just as you would for a standard mat.

To Draw a Circle Locate the two sides and the bottom of the circle by measuring in from the edges of the mat board. Locate the center of the circle. Use a compass or a template to draw the circle on the mat board. To construct a makeshift compass, stick a pin in the center of the circle. Tie one end of a string to the pin and tie the other end to a pencil. Adjust the length of the string until it is right for the circle you want to draw.

83

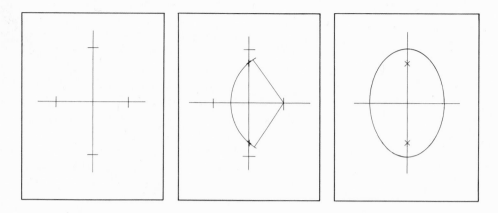

To Draw an Ellipse Locate the two sides and the top and bottom of the ellipse by measuring in from the edges of the mat board. Draw horizontal and vertical lines through the center of the ellipse. The longer line is the major axis. The shorter one is the minor axis. The two foci of the ellipse are located on the major axis, and you must find them before you can draw the ellipse.

To find the foci, use a compass or construct a makeshift one. Set the compass at half the length of the major axis. Then place the point of the compass at one end of the minor axis and draw an arc. This arc will intersect the major axis in two places and these will be the foci.

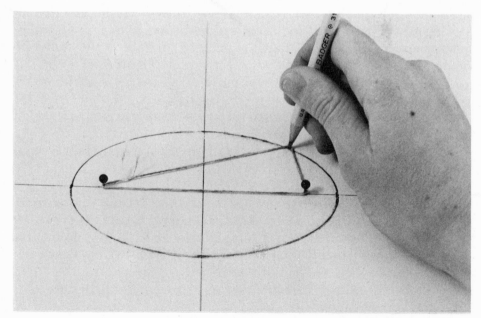

Completed mat with elliptical window. The mat is rag board with brown paper dry mounted on the front surface. The second-hand frame is oak with a thin gold-leafed liner.

Firmly position a push pin, thumbtack, or map tack in each of the foci and a third one at one end of the minor axis. Tie a length of string in a loop which fits tightly around the three pins. Remove the top pin and place the point of your pencil there instead. Then move the pencil around the two foci keeping the string taut. It will trace an ellipse.

To Cut a Curved Window with a Mat Knife   You can cut the window from the front of the mat board or from the back. Small windows or tight curves are more easily cut from the front of the mat, your hand being outside the curve. But to cut from the front you must also draw the opening on the front, and it is easy to accidentally mark or scratch the surface of the mat board. If you are cutting the window from the front of the board, place a soft cloth or tissue under your hand to keep from scratching the mat, and slant the handle of the mat knife away from the window. If you are cutting the window from the back, slant the knife toward the window. Insert the blade in the mat board. Lock your wrist in position and pull the mat knife toward you, following the curve of the circle. Cut as far as possible without stopping. Then without removing the mat knife, lift the mat slightly from the table and turn it to a position where you can cut the next portion of the circle. Cut slowly and follow the line you have drawn exactly. Any deviation will show on the front of the mat. When you reach the end of the circle, it is crucial to meet the beginning of the line exactly — if you are off at all, there will be a bump in the bevel.

To Cut a Curved Window with a Dexter Cutter You must cut the window from the back with the Dexter cutter because the cutter will scratch the surface of the mat if you try to cut from the front. The instructions are otherwise the same as those above, except that you must *push* the Dexter cutter along the cutting line. It takes some practice to cut a smooth even curve with a Dexter cutter.

DOUBLE MATS A double mat is actually two mats for the same picture. The windows of both mats usually have bevelled edges and the outer dimensions of the two mats are the same. The window of the bottom mat is smaller than the opening in the top mat, so that the bottom mat is visible around the picture. You can even cut three or more mats for the same picture if you wish, each mat with a larger window than the one below.

Draw a diagram of the two mats together.

Measure the artwork to determine the dimensions of the window opening in the bottom mat — the smaller opening. Note the horizontal and vertical dimensions of the window on your sketch.

Decide how much of the bottom mat should show. Most double mats have ¼" to ½" of the bottom mat showing. (Usually the amount of the bottom mat showing is the same on all four sides, but you can alter this for effect.) If you want only a very small amount of the bottom mat showing, remember that the bevel of the bottom mat will take up ⅟₁₆" of your measurement, so the actual colored surface showing will be ⅟₁₆" less than your measurement. Also remember that any discrepancies in the cutting of either mat will be more noticeable if only a narrow band of color separates them.

Add the horizontal dimension of the bottom window to the margin on either side to find the horizontal measurement of the window

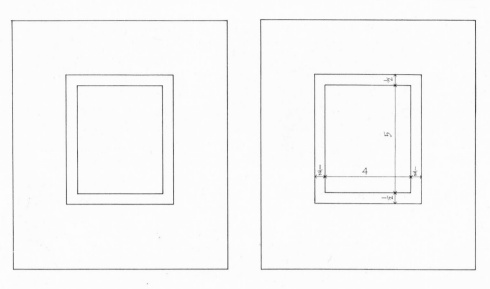

of the top mat. Add the vertical dimension of the bottom window to the margin on the top and bottom to find the vertical dimension of the window of the top mat.

Note these dimensions on your diagram.

At this point if you are using a third mat repeat this last step to determine its window size.

Decide how wide you would like the margins of the top mat to be. It may be helpful to place a sample of the frame next to the samples of the two mats. Note the measurements of the margins of the top mat on your diagram.

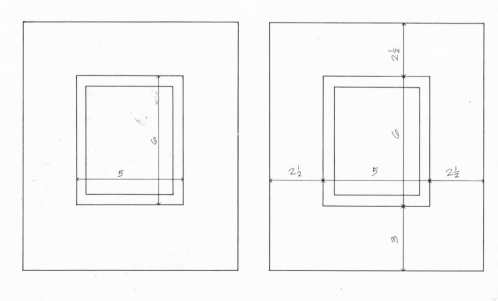

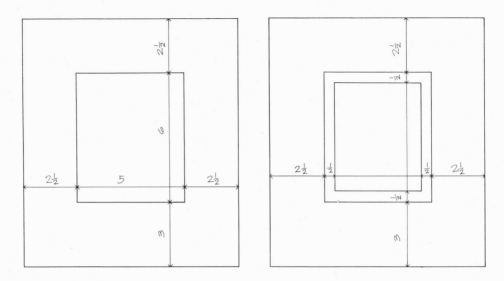

Add the horizontal window measurement of the top mat to the two side margins of the top mat to determine the overall horizontal dimensions of the mats. Add the vertical window dimension of the top mat to the top and bottom margins of the top mat to find the overall vertical dimension of the mats.

At this point draw a separate diagram of the top mat and note the outside dimensions, window measurements, margins, and color of the mat.

The only measurements left to determine are the widths of the margins of the bottom mat. On each side of the mat, add the margin

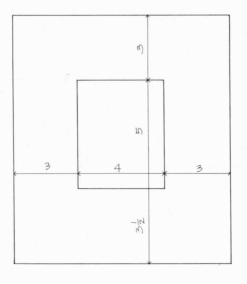

of the top mat to the amount of the bottom mat which is to show through the window of the top one. This gives you the margins of the bottom mat.

As a double check, add the window measurements of the bottom mat to the margins of the bottom mat. The overall dimensions should equal the overall dimensions you have already determined for the top mat.

Draw a separate diagram showing the bottom mat only. Note outside dimensions, window dimensions, margins, and color of the mat.

Cutting Double Mats Cut each mat following the instructions for cutting a standard mat. After they are cut, you may stick the mats together with double-stick tape so that they won't slip out of alignment.

FABRIC-COVERED MATS
TOOLS
> *Push pins, map tacks, or thumbtacks*
> *Razor blade or sharp mat knife blade*
> *Elmer's glue or other white glue*

The fabric most commonly used for covering mats is silk, but any number of fabrics can be used with satisfactory results. Very bulky fabrics are usually hard to work with and tend to bulge at the wrong places. Very loose-weave fabrics like burlap sometimes don't cover the mat satisfactorily. Velvet crushes under glass, but it can be used with tiny rag board or balsa wood spacers providing a space between the mat and the glass. Velveteen can be a problem because the nap separates where it is folded around the bevel and exposes the backing. Shiny fabrics should be carefully chosen because they sometimes compete with the artwork for attention. Fabrics that fray easily are not satisfactory.

Cut the mat and try it on the artwork to make sure it is the right size.

Cut a piece of fabric 3″ to 4″ larger than the mat in each direction.

Place the fabric right-side-down on a clean cutting surface.

Place the mat face-down on the fabric. Make sure that the grain of the fabric is not crooked and if there is a pattern on the fabric, make sure it is right-side-up on the mat.

Place pins in the corners of the mat opening, stretching the fabric slightly. Place pins at the outside corners of the mat, continuing to stretch the fabric slightly and making sure the grain of the fabric is still parallel with the mat.

89

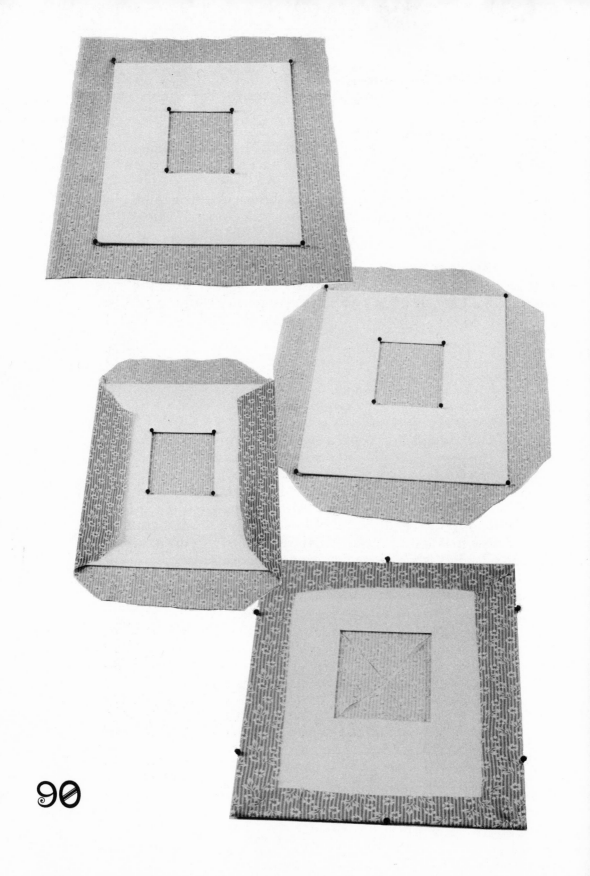

The completed fabric-covered mat. A beige fabric with a tiny floral pattern was chosen to complement the brown tones in an old photograph. The frame is an old oak one that was purchased at a garage sale, stripped, varnished, and rubbed to a smooth finish.

Cut across the outer corners of the fabric as shown.

Spread a thin layer of white glue on the back of the mat board along one side. Pull the pins along that side and fold the fabric over the mat board, keeping the grain straight and the fabric taut. As you pull the fabric around the mat board, also pull it toward the corners.

Glue the opposite side next; then the two remaining sides.

Set pins around the outside of the mat board to keep it from moving.

Use a sharp mat knife blade or razor blade to trim off any excess fabric that would get in the way when you fold the fabric around the window opening.

Cut an X from corner to corner of the window with a very sharp blade.

Wrap the fabric around the window edges. Glue opposite sides first, maintaining tension on the fabric and making sure the grain is straight.

Glue the two remaining sides.

Check the corners of the mat window. If necessary use a toothpick to apply glue in the corner. Then press the fabric into place.

Weight the mat and allow it to dry overnight.

MATS WITH PAINTED BEVELS Painting the bevel of a mat window is not hard, but it is a slow and exacting job. Acrylic paints are excellent and some marker pens work as well, and you might try other paints, chalks, or crayons that you have around. Whatever you decide to use, experiment first with a scrap of the same type of mat board you plan to paint, to get the feel of it and to make sure the paint covers well and doesn't run.

You will need very strong light because you must be able to see the edge of the bevel clearly. The paint should not be runny or it will tend to spread on the surface of the mat. It should be just thin enough to spread with a brush.

Hold the mat face-up in front of you. Reach through the window from below and apply the paint with downward strokes.

If your mat is 100 percent rag board, you can shave off any mistakes with a razor blade.

FRENCH MATS
TOOLS
Watercolors
Pencil
Ruling pen — available at art supply stores
Paintbrush

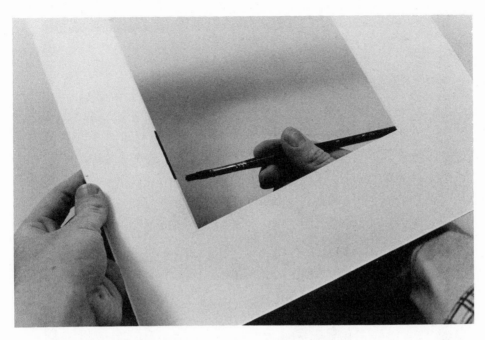

Painting the bevel of a mat.

A traditional French mat has several colored lines around the window, one or more bands of pale color, and sometimes a narrow strip of metal leaf. French mats may look complex to design and difficult to execute, but once you know a few simple tricks, it is much easier than it looks.

Designing the Mat If the mat is for an old piece of art, the colors should be very pale so that they won't overpower the artwork, which is usually faded and dulled with age, and they should not be pure colors but mixtures. They may sometimes be dulled by the addition of a little brown or gray. All the colors used in the mat should be similar, but each line is usually a slightly different color. In the context of the mat several lines close together will make the colors appear brighter than they actually are and even slight color variations will show up.

It is the subtle variations in both color and spacing that make the French mat so intriguing to look at. And the only way to arrive at a suitable arrangement for your particular piece of artwork is to experiment. On scrap pieces of mat board try different line weights, arrangements, and colors. If you can, go to a museum or gallery where you can see some French mats. You will find that there are usually several different line weights in each mat, and often the heavier lines are

93

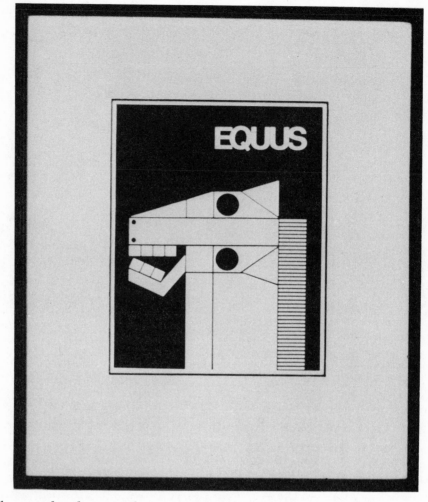

The completed mat with a painted bevel.

toward the outside. The spaces between the lines will all be different except occasionally where the repetition of the same spacing provides extra emphasis.

Rag board is normally used for French mats because artwork that requires a French mat is usually valuable. Also, the surface of the rag board takes paint better than a wood pulp board, and the bevel of the rag board is the same color as the surface. The bevel of a wood pulp board is always a different color from the surface and this can detract from the fine linework of a French mat.

If you decide to use a wood pulp board for a French mat, test a scrap of it first to see how the color looks on it and to be sure ruled lines don't bleed onto the surface of the board.

Four designs for a French mat. The inner pair of lines in each diagram represents the bevel of the mat.

Painting a French Mat   Cut the mat just as you would cut a standard mat. If it is hard for you to visualize the size of the mat margins before you have painted the mat, cut the mat a little larger than you think you will want it. You can always trim the edges later to make it exactly the size you want.

Draw the lines very lightly in pencil on the front of the mat. Measure from the top of the bevel and make the lines exactly the same distance from the bevel on all four sides.

Mix the colors for the wide band. I find a styrofoam egg carton easiest to mix colors in — you can mix several colors at once. Thin the water-color until it barely shows any color when you brush it onto the surface of the mat.

Use a soft bristle brush, preferably one that is not quite so wide as the band you are painting. Hold the mat at an angle so that the color doesn't puddle as you put it on. Brush it on quickly; it will leave a line if it dries before you get back to the starting point. Don't worry if you go over the line a little here and there — you will draw a line along the edge of the band later.

Set the mat aside to dry.

Apply as many more coats as you need to get the color you want. The reason for applying color in several coats is to prevent streaking or dense areas of color. The color will be more uniform with several applications.

If you have more colored bands in your mat, paint these next.

If you are using a metal leaf band in your mat, apply it next. The adhesive-backed metal foil is easy to use: simply peel the protective covering off the back and put it lightly in place on the mat. If you want a strip that is thinner than the roll of foil, use a metal straight-edge and a mat knife to trim off the excess after you have placed it on the mat. Allow the strips to overlap at the corners. Then at each corner use a razor blade or sharp mat knife to make a mitered cut through both layers of foil. Remove the scrap pieces and you will have a perfectly mitered corner.

Drawing the lines on a French mat with a ruling pen.

Practice with the ruling pen before you begin work with it on the mat. The water-color solution for the ruled lines should be just as thin as it was for the painted band, but the color can be more concentrated. With the brush, pick up a little water-color and place it in the ruling pen. Use a metal straightedge with a padded bottom or a draftsman's triangle with a raised edge. If the bottom surface of the straightedge is in contact with the mat, capillary action will draw the water-color under the straightedge and ruin your mat. Test the ruling pen on a piece of scrap mat board to see if the line is the right width. Adjust the pen to make the line wider or narrower. Practice drawing with it. If you press too hard, the sharp point of the pen will cut through the top surface of the mat board and the edge of the line will be fuzzy.

Place your straightedge on the side of the line away from the window. Draw your first ruled line all the way around the window, going over it again if it isn't dark enough. Go slowly and refill the pen as often as necessary to get a uniform line.

Allow the first line to dry before you go on to the next one. While you're waiting, you can mix and test more colors for the rest of the mat.

12 Glass and Acrylic

THE GLASS OR ACRYLIC in the frame provides a clear protective covering over the front of the artwork, protecting against dirt, moisture, and fingerprints. Both glass and acrylic have advantages and disadvantages.

Glass is simple to clean and does not scratch easily. It is commonly available at reasonable prices. However, glass breaks easily, which is of special concern if the picture is to be moved frequently or shipped long distances. Replacing a large piece of glass can be expensive, so breakage is especially bothersome with very large pieces.

Large sheets of glass are very heavy, so you may have to provide extra support for the picture. *And glass is dangerous.* You can injure yourself seriously handling even a small piece, and it breaks easily if a frame is knocked off the wall.

Acrylic doesn't break and is lightweight, and so is preferable to glass for use in large frames and for pictures to be hung in children's rooms; however, acrylic scratches easily and requires special cleaners, and it builds up static electricity that attracts dust. Acrylic is not suitable for large clip systems under tension, such as the Eubank Frame, since tension causes the acrylic to bend.

Both glass and acrylic come with a regular or a non-glare surface. Non-glare glass and acrylic do not reflect light, so they are used whenever the light from a nearby window or lamp would reflect from the surface of regular glass or acrylic. The non-glare surface appears frosty in comparison with the regular, so before you decide to use it, place a sample of non-glare and a sample of regular on the artwork and observe the difference. The non-glare usually dulls colors a little and makes sharp lines appear a bit fuzzy — you lose some of the clarity of regular glass or acrylic. For this reason, I never recommend the non-glare for etchings or drawings with fine linework, pictures with subtle or interesting colors, or any original artwork. Non-glare glass or acrylic is also unsatisfactory for artwork with two or more mats because the image becomes fuzzier as the glass or acrylic is moved away from it.

GLASS Glass for framing is available in picture weight, single weight, or double weight. Picture weight is $\frac{1}{16}''$ thick, and is fine for small pictures but too easily broken in sheets over 24" x 30". Single weight, about $\frac{3}{32}''$ thick, is commonly used on anything less than 30" x 40". In sizes larger than this, it too is easily broken. Double weight glass, $\frac{1}{8}''$ thick, should be used for anything larger than 30" x 40".

You have the choice of buying glass cut to your specifications or buying standard-size glass and cutting it yourself. I recommend always buying your glass cut to the size you need. *Cutting glass yourself is dangerous* — tiny slivers fly from the glass as you score it and as you break it; *you can cut yourself very badly handling it;* and once you have cut it you are faced with the problem of safely disposing of the scraps. If there is a charge for having glass cut for you, it will be small.

Glass can be purchased at frame stores, hardware stores, or glass companies. Frame stores normally stock picture weight and/or single weight. Hardware stores usually carry single weight. Double weight glass and extremely large sizes can usually be found only at a glass company. Some frame stores also carry oval glass and domed oval glass. Whenever you buy glass, be sure that it has no wrinkles, bubbles, or scratches, and make sure that it does not have a greenish cast that would tint your artwork (all glass will look green from the edge, but it should not appear green when you place it on a white background).

Cutting Glass
   TOOLS
      Glass cutter
      Straightedge
      Watercolor pen such as a Flair pen
      Emery cloth

Cut the glass the same size as the mat and backing. If you are cutting it to fit an already assembled frame, measure the opening in the back of the frame and subtract $\frac{1}{8}''$ from each dimension. This allows enough clearance for the glass to slip into the frame without scraping the sides, and it allows a slight margin for error in cutting.

If you haven't cut glass before, it takes some practice to learn the correct amount of pressure to use and to cut a straight line. So experiment with some scrap pieces of glass to get the feel of it.

Remember that glass is dangerous. Wear goggles or glasses to protect your eyes from tiny slivers of glass as you score and break the piece. Handle the glass gently and slowly. And if you expect to cut several pieces, buy a pair of thin leather gloves. They protect your hands from nicks or scratches and give you a better grip when you carry the glass.

Place the glass flat on a clean cutting surface.

Mark the cutting lines on the surface of the glass with a fine-tip watercolor pen such as a Flair pen.

Scoring the glass with a glass cutter.

Score the glass with the glass cutter. Pull the glass cutter toward you exerting moderate pressure. You may use a straightedge as a guide or just draw the cutter freehand across the line. The cutter should score the entire length of the line. If it skips any portion, the glass will not break cleanly. It dulls the cutter to go back over the same area again, so get in the habit of scoring it evenly the first time.

The score begins to mend itself immediately, so the glass will be more difficult to break later than right after you score it.

Move the glass to the edge of the table with the score running perpendicular to the edge of the table. Hold the glass as shown with thumbs on top and one hand on either side of the scored line. Holding the glass firmly, break it along the scored line.

If the glass does not break along the line, it may not have been scored evenly. Turn it around and try breaking it from the other end. If you are going to be cutting a lot of glass you may find it worthwhile

Breaking the glass.

to invest in a pair of glass pliers to be used for grasping and breaking off thin slivers.

Finish the edges of the glass by sanding them with emery cloth. This is not necessary, but you will be less likely to cut yourself on glass that is sanded.

Handling Glass   A large thin sheet of picture glass in a horizontal position can't support its own weight. It will begin to bow in the middle and will probably break. Carry glass vertically. It is best to carry it only by the top edge so that if it breaks while you are carrying it, your arm will not be under it. Whenever possible, carry the glass with a backing the same size to give it added support.

Do not pick up a piece of glass by the ends or by the corners. To lift it from the table, grasp it in the center of the long edge. Allow the opposite edge to rest on the table — the entire edge, not just one corner of it. Lift the glass to a vertical position. If it is necessary to move it, keep it in a vertical position, holding it by the top edge. To put it down again, rest the bottom edge on the table and lower the top edge until the glass rests flat on the table.

Handle the glass with gloves or paper towels to keep from getting slivers in your hands and to keep your fingerprints off it once you have started cleaning it.

101

Cleaning Glass Leave the glass flat on the table to clean it. Do not stand it up in a vertical position, as the slight pressure you exert in cleaning it may be enough to break it.

Spray the top surface with diluted glass cleaner (about 1 part glass cleaner to 10 parts water). The reason for diluting it is that full-strength cleaner leaves a film on the surface of the glass. Use pieces of newspaper to clean it — newspaper doesn't leave lint and the ink contains chemicals that aid in the cleaning action. Keep using fresh pieces of newspaper. Turn the glass over and clean the other side. Pay special attention to the edges: they are the hardest part to get clean. To see if there are any smudges or fingerprints remaining, place a lamp so that it glares off the surface of the glass; any dirt will show up in the glare. Never lift a sheet of glass above your head to see if it is clean.

Tape or labels on glass can easily be removed with a razor blade or mat knife blade held at a low angle; a blade held perpendicular to the surface of the glass may scratch it.

After cleaning the glass, brush off any remaining lint or dust with a soft brush or lint-free cloth.

ACRYLIC Acrylic can be purchased at plastic companies, some frame stores, and some hardware stores. It may be sold by the trade names Plexiglas, Perspex, Acrylite, or Lucite. It varies in price, but usually costs half again to twice as much as glass.

Acrylic is available in non-glare and regular surfaces. For particularly valuable or fragile artwork, ultraviolet-filtering acrylic is also available. Both the non-glare and the ultraviolet-filtering acrylic are more expensive than the regular.

You can buy acrylic cut to size or buy a large sheet and cut it yourself. It isn't hard to cut. It just requires a special tool, makes a lot of noise, and produces a lot of plastic shavings.

Whenever you are buying acrylic cut to size, let the person cutting it know that it is for a frame and therefore must be cut exactly to size. It is difficult to trim just a little bit off the edge of a piece of an acrylic sheet if it is slightly too large.

Some acrylic manufacturers emboss the name of the company in one corner of the sheet. Obviously you don't want acrylic for a frame cut from that corner.

Cutting Acrylic There are two ways to cut acrylic. You can cut it with a saw or you can scribe it with a plastic cutting tool and then break it. If you will be gluing the edges of the acrylic or if the edges will not be covered by a frame, cut it with a saw since the cut will be smoother. Otherwise, either method is satisfactory.

Acrylic should be cut the same size as the mat and backing. If you are cutting it for a frame that is already assembled, measure the back opening of the frame and subtract ⅛" to determine the size of the acrylic.

When you buy the acrylic it will have a protective plastic or paper covering on it. Since the surface scratches so easily, this covering should not be removed until the last minute, so cut the acrylic with the covering still in place.

Mark cutting lines on the acrylic with a straightedge and a pencil. If you are cutting several pieces from one large sheet, draw a diagram first to determine the most efficient way to cut them. Remember that each cut you make must go all the way across the piece you are cutting from.

TO CUT ACRYLIC BY SCRIBING AND BREAKING
TOOLS
Metal straightedge
Plastic cutter

Hold the straightedge along the cutting line with the straightedge over the piece you intend to use. Draw the cutting tool toward you along the straightedge. Apply only light pressure on the first cut — this will make a groove that will be easy to follow on subsequent cuts. Make several cuts along the same line using moderate pressure, and keep cutting until you have cut about halfway through.

Position the scored line along the edge of the table. Hold the acrylic sheet firmly on the table with one hand and apply pressure to the extended portion with the other hand. It will snap along the scored line. If it doesn't break make several more cuts with the cutting tool and try to break it again.

If the piece you are breaking off is very narrow, break it the same way as glass. Place the score line perpendicular to the edge of the table. Grasp the piece with both hands, thumbs on top, one hand on either side of the score, and break it.

TO CUT ACRYLIC WITH A SAW
TOOLS
Table saw, circular saw, or saber saw

If you are using a table saw or circular saw, a blade used for cutting wood is not satisfactory since it will chip the acrylic. Instead purchase a blade made specifically for cutting plastics, or a blade for making finish cuts on plywood or veneers, or a metal cutting blade.

103

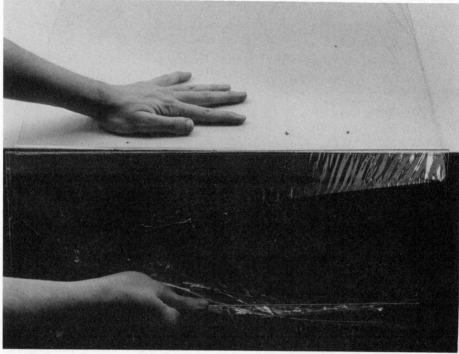

Breaking acrylic.

Clamp the acrylic to a table or work bench so it doesn't vibrate when you cut with a circular saw or saber saw.

Finishing the Edge of the Acrylic   Place the acrylic in a clamp or vise so you can use both hands to finish the edge. Scrape the edge with a wood scraper or the back edge of a hacksaw blade or file it with a flat file to remove saw marks.

Then sand with finer and finer grit wet-or-dry papers. Use a #180 to #220 first, then #280 to #320, and finally #400 to #500. Dip the paper in water occasionally to reduce the heat from sanding and to prevent the paper from clogging.

Polish the edge with jeweler's rouge or with a buffing attachment for an electric drill. You can buy buffing compound along with the buffing attachment or substitute toothpaste or silver polish.

Cleaning Acrylic   To clean a sheet of acrylic, use a dilute solution of mild dishwashing liquid or a commercial plastic cleaner. Spray it on and wipe the surface clean with a clean cotton flannel or jersey cloth or a Photographer's Wipe. Do not use glass cleaners and do not use newspaper as you would with glass.

Place the acrylic flat on the table and remove the protective covering from one side. Clean that side. Remove any lint or dust with a lint-free cloth or Photographer's Wipe. Place the artwork and backing face-down on the clean side of the acrylic and proceed with your frame. You can clean the other side of the acrylic after it is in the frame.

Whenever you work with acrylic, be careful not to slide it on the work surface since it scratches very easily.

13 Backings

THERE MUST BE a stiff backing in the frame to support the picture from behind, holding it flat against the mat and glass, and protecting it from scratches, tears, and dust. The backing should be the full size of the mat and glass, since it can't function properly as a stiff support if it does not reach all the way to the edge of the frame.

BACKING MATERIALS

Corrugated Cardboard   This is the board that corrugated cartons are made of. It is acidic and therefore harmful to the artwork over long periods of time, so you may want to insert an acid-free backing between the cardboard and the art. Cardboard can be purchased in sheets or cut to size from a picture frame shop, or you can scrounge a cardboard carton from a furniture or other store and cut your own backing.

Fome-Cor   This is a polystyrene foam center coated on both sides with white paper or brown kraft paper. It comes in several thicknesses but the most common one for framing is ¼". Fome-Cor is thicker and stiffer than cardboard so it is a more satisfactory backing for larger pictures, those over 24" x 30". White Fome-Cor comes with a shiny surface or a dull surface. The dull surface is better for dry mounting. Fome-Cor with very small-grain foam cuts better than Fome-Cor with large-celled foam (this is only important if you are framing so that the edge of the Fome-Cor will be visible). The white coating on Fome-Cor is acid-free, so it provides more protection than corrugated cardboard. However, if you want archival quality framing you must use rag board between the Fome-Cor and the artwork. Fome-Cor is commonly used as a backing for stretching small pieces of fabric or needlework. White-surface Fome-Cor should be used as a backing behind artwork on thin white paper. Fome-Cor can be purchased at art supply stores or framing stores. It comes in sheets 30" x 40" and 40" x 60".

Plywood and Masonite These backings are extremely acidic and they are also heavy. If you use a plywood or masonite backing, you will need to choose an extra strong frame and you will probably have to take extra measures to hang the picture. These backings are commonly used when a rigid backing is needed for stretching.

Mat Board Mat board is used when the color of the backing is important — when you are floating paper or fabric artwork on a background, or framing a paper cutout or a print on clear acetate. It is not stiff enough to be used as the only backing for anything larger than about a 9″ x 12″, so another stiff backing is usually used behind it. It can be purchased at art supply or framing stores.

Uncoated Cardboards Chipboard and Upson board are solid cardboard backings that come in various thicknesses from ⅟₃₂″ to ¼″. They are commonly used for stretching small pieces of fabric or needlework, and for backings in frames, but they are hard to cut and acidic. I recommend using Fome-Cor instead. Both products are available at art supply stores.

TO CUT BACKINGS
TOOLS
Mat knife
Straightedge
Pencil

First determine the dimensions for the backing. It should be the same size as the mat or glass. If you are cutting the backing to fit a frame that is already assembled, measure the opening in the back of the frame and subtract ⅛″ from each dimension. This allows enough clearance for the backing to expand and contract naturally without pushing against the side of the frame and buckling.

If the backing is cardboard or Fome-Cor, place the board on a clean cutting surface and draw the perimeter with a straightedge and pencil.

Use the straightedge as a guide and cut with a sharp mat knife. You can usually cut through mat board, corrugated cardboard, or Fome-Cor in one cut, but it may take several cuts to cut through the heavier chipboard and Upson boards.

If the backing is plywood or masonite, lay out the perimeter on the board with a pencil and straightedge. Check to make sure the corners are square. The quickest way to do this is to measure the two diagonals. If they are equal, the corners are right angles. Cut the board with a handsaw or a table saw.

107

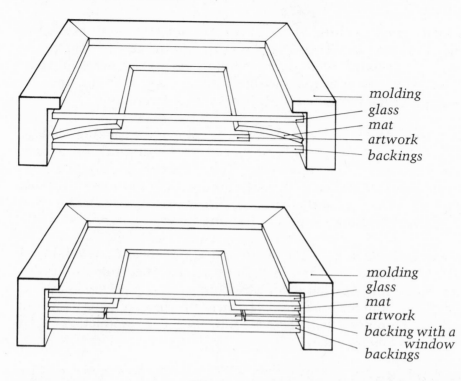

molding
glass
mat
artwork
backings

molding
glass
mat
artwork
backing with a
window
backings

TO CUT A WINDOW IN A BACKING A backing with a window solves a special problem — holding a piece of thick artwork in place in a frame with a mat. The item might be a mounted poster or a stretched piece of cloth or needlework which you want to mat. If the outer dimension of the mat is larger than the outer dimension of the artwork, the mat will bend when it is put into the frame. You need to put a backing the same thickness as the artwork under the mat so that the mat will stay flat in the frame.

Cut the mat first. Then choose a backing board about the same thickness as the artwork. Cut the perimeter the same size as the outside of the mat. Place the artwork face-up on the backing with the mat on top. Line up the edges of the mat and backing, and line up the artwork with the mat window. When all three are aligned, remove the mat and trace the outline of the artwork on the backing with a pencil. Cut the hole in the backing using a mat knife and straightedge. The artwork should fit easily into the opening in the backing. You still need a rigid backing, so when you assemble the frame, use regular cardboard or Fome-Cor behind the backing with a window.

108 **PROTECTIVE BACKINGS** Since most stiff backings are acidic, you may want to use a protective backing in the frame between the artwork and the stiff backing. An acidic backing would be in contact with the entire area of the artwork, so it is sensible to consider using a protective backing even if you are using an acidic mat, which will affect only the edges around the cut window.

Acid-free Backings   The acid-free backing may be rag paper, two-ply rag board, or four-ply rag board. All serve the same purpose, but the thicker the rag the longer it will be effective.

Rag paper is also called Barrier Paper, Process Art Paper, or Neutral pH Paper. Rag board is also called museum board. Both can be purchased at art supply and framing stores.

Cut rag board the same way you cut a stiff backing. To cut rag paper, trace around the stiff backing and cut the paper with scissors.

Non-porous Backings   A non-porous backing prevents any acid from the stiff backing from traveling through to the artwork. It is used for the best possible protection against acid and is inserted between the stiff backing and the acid-free backing. It must be used in addition to the acid-free backing, not in lieu of it, because it can trap moisture against the artwork if framed in contact with it. The non-porous backing can be Mylar or aluminum foil. Either is effective but Mylar is preferable because it doesn't condense moisture so readily as foil.

You probably have aluminum foil around the house already. Mylar can be purchased at art supply stores or mail-ordered from Talas.

14 Attaching Artwork to the Mat or Backing

IF THE ARTWORK, glass, and backing are all the same size and if there is no mat, the art doesn't need to be attached to anything: the pressure of the glass will hold it in place. In other cases, the artwork must be attached either to the mat or to the backing to keep it from slipping out of position inside the frame.

Artwork attached to the mat is likely to get punctured or torn in framing or subsequent reframing. Therefore anything of value should be attached to a rag board backing.

ATTACHING ARTWORK TO A MAT
MATERIALS
Masking tape or drafting tape
Linen tape

Linen tape is an acid-free tape made for bookbinding and commonly used in picture framing. It is archivally safe. It is quickly and easily applied and can be removed with a Q-tip dipped in water. It is very strong and forms a secure and lasting bond. It has three disadvantages: it is thick and therefore likely to show behind very thin paper; it curls slightly and of course curls the edge of the paper with it; and it is stronger than the artwork, so that the art will tear before the tape will. For most items being framed these disadvantages are minor, and linen tape is an easy and perfectly satisfactory method of attaching the artwork. It should not be used for extremely old, fragile, or valuable items.

There are two acceptable substitutes for linen tape: One is the gummed paper from the end of a sheet of postage stamps, which is archivally safe and can be used just like linen tape for attaching artwork to a mat or backing.

Micro-pore tape, a first aid tape, is also acid-free but may react with the paper over a period of years to form harmful chemicals. Since it is pressure-sensitive, it is difficult to remove from the artwork. It is satisfactory only for artwork that is not valuable.

Other pressure-sensitive tapes — such as clear tapes and masking tape — should not be used on artwork; they discolor the paper with time and can be difficult to remove.

To attach the artwork to the back of the mat

Place the artwork face-up on a clean work surface.

Place a piece of masking tape face-up under the two sides and the top of the artwork, extending about 2″ beyond the edge.

Place the mat over the art and position it exactly as you want it. Then press down on the mat to stick it to the masking tape. The masking tape should barely hold the artwork in place. Don't stick it

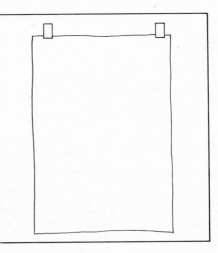

down tight. When you do this take care not to place your fingers directly on the front of the mat, as the oils in your skin can stain the mat in time. Use a paper napkin or cloth to handle the face of the mat.

Turn the mat over.

Use two pieces of linen tape to attach the picture along the top edge. The tape should be placed near each corner. If you feel a third piece is necessary, place it in the center of the top edge. Most of the tape should be on the mat — only about ⅛" should extend over the edge of the artwork. Moisten the linen tape and hold it tightly in place for about 30 seconds to make it stick tightly. The picture should be taped to the mat only at the top because if it is fastened all the way around it can't expand and contract naturally and may buckle or tear instead.

Remove the masking tape. It will stain the artwork if it is left on, and the extra tape can cause buckling.

HINGING THE MAT TO THE BACKING
MATERIALS
Linen tape or masking tape

Place the backing face-up on a clean work surface and place the mat face-down with the top edge of the mat touching the top edge of the backing.

Tape along the adjoining edges with linen tape or masking tape.

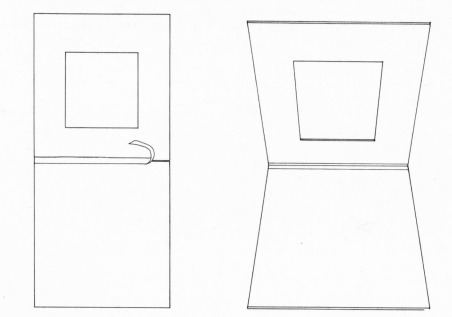

Masking tape slips out of alignment easily, so use linen tape if you have it available.

Fold the mat down into place.

If you are framing something for display with only a mat and backing and you are not using archival procedures, you may use double-stick tape to attach mat to backing. Take care not to put the tape where it might come in contact with the artwork.

ATTACHING ARTWORK TO THE BACKING There are three ways to attach artwork to a backing. You can use linen tape, acid-free rice paper and archival paste, or rag paper corners similar to old-fashioned photo corners. For most artwork, the linen tape is perfectly satisfactory. For attaching very thin paper, or fragile or valuable artwork, the rice paper hinges and archival paste are preferable. Rag paper corners can be used when the artwork is fairly stiff and you don't want any tape or paste touching it.

Attaching Artwork to the Backing with Linen Tape
MATERIALS
> *Linen tape*

Hinge the mat to the backing as described above.

Fold the mat out away from the backing. Place the art on the backing face-up, and put the mat back in place. Position the artwork as you want it. Then lay a clean piece of paper on the artwork and place a weight on the paper to hold the artwork in place.

Lift the mat out away from the backing again. Use two small pieces of linen tape to attach the artwork — one piece near each

Attaching artwork to backing with linen tape

113

corner on the top edge. Put a third piece in the center of the top edge if you feel it's needed. Stick the tape to the *back* surface of the paper with the sticky side up and only about ⅛" of the tape in contact with the artwork. The rest of the piece of tape should extend above the top edge of the artwork. Then place another piece of tape, sticky side down, across the first one to hold it in place. Hold the tape firmly in place for a couple of minutes to make it stick. This way there is no tape in contact with the front of the artwork.

Attaching the Artwork to the Backing with Rice Paper Hinges and Archival Paste

MATERIALS

> *Acid-free rice paper*
>
> *Archival paste — You can order it in powdered form from Talas or Twin City Moulding and Supply, or mix your own using the following recipe. The rice paste only keeps for about a week once it is mixed up and the ingredients may be hard to find, so unless you are mounting several pieces of artwork, you will find it easier and more economical to use the paste powder.*

TO MAKE RICE PASTE

INGREDIENTS

> *3 tablespoons rice starch (from an Oriental grocery)*
> *¾ cup water*
> *2 teaspoons clear Karo syrup*
> *¾ teaspoon glycerol (from a drug store)*
> *5 teaspoons stiff clear gelatin*
> *A few drops of thymol dissolved in ethanol (from a druggist or chemical supply house)*

Slowly add the water to the rice starch, stirring constantly.

Heat the mixture in a double boiler continuing to stir.

Combine the Karo syrup, gelatin, and glycerol and heat in a separate pan.

When the starch and water mixture thickens into a stiff paste, combine it with the syrup mixture, stir it well, and remove it from the heat.

Cool to room temperature stirring occasionally so lumps won't form.

Add thymol.

Store rice paste at room temperature in loosely covered containers. Do not refrigerate it.

TO ATTACH THE ARTWORK   Hinge the mat to the backing. Fold the mat out away from the backing. Lay the art on the backing face-up and put the mat back in place. Position the artwork as you want it in relation to the mat window. Then put a clean piece of paper on the artwork and a weight on the paper to hold the artwork in place.

Lift the mat away from the backing again. Attach the art to the backing along the top edge with two rice paper hinges, one near each corner. Place a third hinge in the center of the top edge if needed.

To attach the hinges: tear a small strip of rice paper about ½" by 1" from your sheet of rice paper. The strip should be torn rather than cut because a torn edge is softer and less likely to show through thin paper.

Apply paste to one side of the hinge along the bottom edge. Slip this edge under the top edge of the artwork and stick it to the back of the paper. Only about ⅛" of the hinge should be in contact with the artwork.

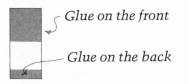

Glue on the front

Glue on the back

Applying paste to a rice paper hinge.

Apply paste to the other side of the hinge along the top edge. Press this part of the hinge onto the backing.

Attach the artwork to the backing only along the top edge.

After you have attached the hinges, place a piece of wax paper under the top edge of the artwork so that paste from the hinges won't stick the art to the backing. Put a piece of wax paper on top of each hinge also. Place some blotter paper over the artwork and the hinges to absorb the moisture as the glue dries, and lay a weighted piece of plywood on top of this.

Let it dry overnight.

Attaching Artwork to the Backing with Rag Paper Corners
MATERIALS
> *Small scraps of rag paper*
> *Linen tape*

Hinge the mat to the backing and fold it out away from the backing. Place the art on the backing face-up and put the mat back in place. Position the artwork as you want it in relation to the mat window. Place a piece of clean paper on the art and put a weight on the paper to hold the work in place. Lift the mat away from the backing again.

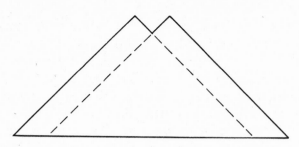

Making a rag paper corner.

Cut the pieces of rag paper as shown. Fold them on the dotted lines. Slip them over the corners of the paper and tape them to the backing with linen tape.

Attaching Artwork to the Backing When All the Edges Will Be Visible

MATERIALS

Linen tape or acid-free rice paper and archival paste

Position the artwork where you want it on the backing. Place a clean piece of paper on the artwork, and put a weight on top of it to keep the artwork from shifting.

Fold two pieces of linen tape in half with the sticky side out and moisten them, or apply paste to one side of two small strips of rice paper and fold them in half.

Slip the hinges under the top two corners of the artwork. Hold the linen tape in place for about a minute to make the tape stick. Place blotting paper and weights over the rice paper hinges and allow the glue to dry for several hours.

ATTACHING A THREE-DIMENSIONAL OBJECT TO A BACKING The most important thing to remember when you are attaching something to a backing is that it should be preserved in its original state and that you should be able to remove the artwork from the frame without injuring it. Methods such as clamping or sewing are therefore preferred to gluing or drilling. The nature of the object will of course determine the most appropriate method of fastening.

Sewing Lightweight three-dimensional objects such as dolls, metal cutouts, or jewelry can be attached to a backing by using nylon monofilament fishing line, available in all sporting goods stores. The objects should be attached in as few places as possible and a separate piece of line should be used at each point. Punch or drill holes in the backing so you can pass the line through the backing, around the object, and again through the backing with a knot behind.

If the object is lightweight and the backing is cloth-covered, you can sew the object to the already stretched cloth backing using only the number of stitches necessary to hold the item in place. If you are attaching a small remnant of cloth to a stretched backing, sew it across the top edge and about 1" down each side.

Clamping   Metal L-screws are commonly used for attaching objects such as plates to a wooden backing. Screw the L's into the backing at three or four points around the perimeter of the object.

An alternative that is often more attractive is to cut very short pieces of picture frame molding and screw them into place around the object. The pieces of molding can be used as is, or covered with fabric.

Magnets   Occasionally you will find a piece that can be successfully held to a backing with magnets. These are adhesive-backed magnetic strips that can be cut to the desired size and stuck to the back of the object being framed. Then a metal strip can be imbedded in the backing. I wouldn't trust the adhesive on the magnetic strips to hold anything very valuable, though.

Screws   Objects that are not valuable and not likely to split can be attached to backings with screws.

15 Mounting

Dry mounting and wet mounting are permanent processes for sticking artwork to a rigid backing. Neither process is foolproof. Original or valuable artwork should never be mounted because it can't be removed and because mounting drastically devalues the artwork.

DRY MOUNTING Dry mounting requires the use of a dry mount press and a tacking iron. Presses vary in size from very small, about 12″ x 16″, to oversized, 4′ x 8′. Some do-it-yourself frame shops have dry mount presses available for customers to use, or you may have access to one through a photographic darkroom or a university art or photography department. You can mount items smaller than 8″ x 10″ at home with an iron, but this is not a good idea for large pieces because the tissue bubbles if it isn't evenly heated.

Purchasing Dry Mount Tissue You can buy dry mount tissue at photography stores and some art supply stores. You will find several different tissues and several manufacturers, but there are basically only three different kinds of tissue.

Standard dry mount tissue, called MT5, is brownish and mounts at 210° to 225° F. It forms a permanent bond and can't be removed. It is used for mounting paper and some photographs but is not satisfactory for resin-coated photographic paper, textured items such as cloth, or very thin white paper.

Tissue for mounting textured objects like fabric or leaves is called Fotoflat. It is white and mounts at around 200°. It bonds under the pressure of a weight after it has been mounted, and the mounted piece can be removed by reheating. However, it is difficult to remove all of the glue from the backing, so the only advantage to being able to remove the piece from the backing is that you can mount it to something else. And since the tissue melts with heat, it is likely to melt if the mounted piece is hung in the direct sunlight. This tissue

118

is fine for thin white papers, although sometimes the glue comes through very thin paper or porous fabric — try a small scrap first.

Tissue for mounting resin-coated photographic paper, called Colormount, Kodak Type 2, or Technal Dry Mounting Tissue, is brownish and mounts at about 200°. This tissue forms a permanent bond and should be used for mounting resin-coated photographs and color photographs. It will also work for anything else that is not textured.

Backings for Dry Mounting   Fome-Cor is the most common backing for dry mounting. It is an attractive backing for posters that are not being framed, as it has a clean white edge when cut. It is stiffer than cardboard or matboard and it is lightweight. The matte-surfaced Fome-Cor is better for mounting than the shiny-surfaced one.

Mat board is often used as a backing for dry mounting when it is important to have a colored border around the artwork without cutting a mat.

Cardboard, chipboard, Upson board, or rag board may also be used as backings for mounting.

All of these are likely to warp to some degree. Fome-Cor warps the least.

If you are mounting something which will then be matted, cut the backing a little larger than the mat. Then after the artwork is mounted and the mat is in place, trim the backing to the same size as the mat.

If you are not going to mat the piece, cut the backing a little larger than the item being mounted. Then after it is mounted, trim the artwork and backing at the same time. If you are mounting a photograph, determine whether it is on resin-coated paper. A resin-coated photograph may be color or black and white, matte or glossy. The identifying characteristic is the resin coating on both the front and back of the photograph that feels like plastic. A resin-coated photograph may be ruined at high temperatures and therefore requires the use of a special tissue which mounts at a low temperature. If you are not sure whether the photograph is resin coated, follow the instructions for mounting resin-coated photographs.

Dry Mounting Anything Except Resin-Coated Photographs
TOOLS AND MATERIALS
Metal straightedge
Mat knife
Dry mount press
Tacking iron (this will be with the press)

119

> *Release paper — A special paper which will not bond to the dry mount tissue. It is used in the press when mounting to keep the tissue from damaging the press. Buy it when you buy the dry mount tissue.*

Set the press at the temperature indicated on your box of tissue. To predry the artwork and the mounting board, place the artwork in the press face-up. If it has been rolled or folded, be sure that all the edges and corners are flat. Lay a clean piece of paper on top. Close the press for about 45 seconds. Remove the artwork from the press and repeat the same procedure with the mounting board. Predrying dries out the artwork and prevents wrinkles or bubbles caused by excess moisture. It also flattens posters that have been rolled or folded and makes them easier to handle.

Tack the dry mount tissue to the back of the artwork. To do this, place the artwork face-down on a clean cutting surface. Place the dry mount tissue over it and line up one edge of the tissue with one edge of the artwork. Tack the tissue to the artwork in the center of that edge by applying pressure with the heated tacking iron and moving it slowly along the edge for 2″ or 3″. To keep the iron clean, place a small piece of release paper over the tissue as you tack.

Trim off the excess mounting tissue to exactly the size of the artwork, using a metal straightedge and a sharp mat knife. If any tissue extends beyond the edge of the artwork it will adhere to things in the press.

The next step is to tack the artwork to the mounting board. Position the work face-up on the mounting board leaving at least an inch of border all around. This border insures that the work will not slide off the board even if it should shift a little as you work with it. Lay a piece of paper over the artwork (so that the iron won't scratch it) and tack in the same place as before. This time the heat from the tacking iron will stick the tissue to the backing.

Now you are ready to seal the art to the mounting board. Place the artwork and the backing face-up in the press. Put a piece of release paper over the artwork and a piece of clean wrapping paper over the release paper. Make sure both sheets of paper are clean. Any wrinkles, hairs, or grains of dirt can make an impression in the surface of a photograph or other artwork.

Close the press for 45 seconds unless you are mounting a colored photograph, in which case close it for 30 seconds.

If your artwork is larger than the press, mount it in several sections. The sections should overlap one another to insure that every bit of the artwork is mounted. It is best to work from the center out on large pieces so that pockets of air won't get trapped in the center.

Place the mounted piece under a weight to cool. Each time you remove the artwork from the press, put it under a weight to cool for a couple of minutes. The weight is important because pressure strengthens the adhesive bond.

Dry Mounting Resin-Coated Photographs

    TOOLS

        Dry mount press
        Tacking iron (with press)
        Plastic cover sheet (with press) or piece of cardboard
        Metal straightedge
        Mat knife
        Release paper

Set the press at the temperature indicated on your box of tissue.

Do not put a resin-coated photograph in the press before you mount the tissue to it. It will curl up.

Place the photograph face-down on a clean cutting surface. Place the mounting tissue on the back of the photograph, lining up one edge of the tissue with one edge of the photograph. Tack the tissue to the photograph in the center of that edge by applying pressure with the heated tacking iron and moving it slowly along the edge for 2" or 3". (If you tack in the center of the photograph, the iron may make an impression in the photograph.) To keep the iron clean, place a small scrap of release paper over the tissue as you tack.

Trim the excess tissue. Trim the other sides of the tissue to exactly the same size as the artwork using a metal straightedge and a sharp mat knife. If any tissue extends beyond the edge of the photograph it will adhere to other things in the press.

To mount the tissue to the back of the photograph, place a piece of clean paper (brown wrapping paper is fine) in the press. Any wrinkles or specks of dirt on the paper will make impressions in the photograph, so inspect it carefully. Place the photograph *face-down* on the brown paper. Place a sheet of release paper on top of the photo, and another sheet of brown paper over that. Only the release paper should be in contact with the mounting tissue since the tissue will adhere to anything else in the press.

Place the special plastic cover sheet on top of everything else. This cover sheet is manufactured especially for use with resin-coated photographs. Its purpose is to keep them from getting too hot too fast. If you don't have one, substitute a piece of cardboard instead. Close the press for 30 seconds. Remove the photograph and place it under the weight to cool for a couple of minutes. The tissue should be uniformly stuck to the back of the photograph. If there are any bubbles or wrinkles in the tissue, replace it in the press for 15 to 30 seconds.

Predry the mounting board by placing it in the press for 30 seconds.

To tack the artwork to the mounting board, place the photograph face-up on the backing, put a piece of release paper over it, and tack along one edge with the heated tacking iron. This will stick the tissue to the backing board.

Now you are ready to mount the photograph to the backing in the press. Place the mounting board and photograph face-up in the press and put the plastic cover sheet (or your substitute piece of cardboard) on the photograph. Make sure it's absolutely clean; any dirt or streaks of glue will mar the surface of the photograph. Lay the sheet of release paper and then the sheet of regular paper on top. Close the press for 30 seconds.

As soon as you remove the photograph from the press, place it under a weight to cool for a couple of minutes. This is extremely important because pressure strengthens the bond as the piece cools.

If the photograph has not adhered to the backing and peels up easily, there is not enough heat reaching it. Try again without the extra cover sheet.

A resin-coated photograph that is larger than the press should never be mounted in sections — the edge of the press will leave a mark in the emulsion.

WET MOUNTING
TOOLS AND MATERIALS
Mounting paste
Metal straightedge
Mat knife
Rubber roller or brayer — available at art supply stores

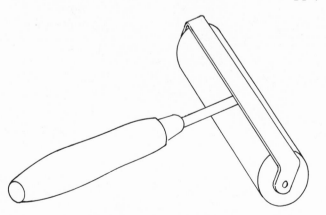

The adhesive for wet mounting is a vegetable paste. There are many pastes available but some cause the paper to stretch when the paste is applied. It then shrinks as it dries, causing the backing to warp. So be sure to purchase a paste made specifically for mounting or one with a label stating that it won't stretch the paper. Art supply stores usually carry mounting paste; two common brands are Yes Glue and Instapaste. Or you can order Record Brand Special Mounting Paste from Twin City Moulding and Supply.

Backings commonly used for wet mounting are Fome-Cor (with a matte surface, not a smooth, glossy one), Upson board, heavy chipboard, or mat board. Any of these backings will probably warp in time.

Cut the backing a little larger than the artwork — about 2″ larger in each direction. Place the artwork face-up on the backing and draw a line around the edge so you will know where to put the paste.

Apply the paste to the mounting board with a piece of scrap mat board, using it like a squeegee to spread the paste thinly over the backing.

Place the artwork face-up on the backing. Smooth it flat with your hands and then roll it flat with a clean rubber roller to remove bubbles and wrinkles.

Weight the piece and allow it to dry overnight.

Trim the backing down to the size you want it.

16 Stretching

ALL PAINTINGS ON CANVAS and most fabric and needlework must be stretched on a rigid support so that the cloth is shown to its best advantage, with all sags, puckers, and wrinkles pulled out.

The support for stretching can be a wooden stretcher frame or the solid backings — plywood, Fome-Cor, or mounting board — described in Chapter 13. Generally the mounting board and Fome-Cor are fine for smaller pieces. Larger items, which are likely to be more difficult to stretch, require the rigidity of a wood support or stretcher frame.

Wood supports, and any mounting boards except Fome-Cor and rag board, are acidic and will discolor the fabric and make it brittle after a few years. This is of special concern when you are using a solid support that is in contact with the entire back surface of the fabric instead of just the edges. So if you intend to keep the piece for several years, you should insert a sheet of rag board between a solid acidic backing and the cloth before you begin stretching. If you use a wood stretcher frame, you can paint it with polyurethane to seal it.

The color of the support will be important if you are stretching very thin fabric or loose-weave cloth like burlap. Insert a piece of mat board, rag board, or paper the appropriate color between the support and the fabric before you begin stretching.

If you are using glass in the frame it is better to use a Fome-Cor or mounting board support rather than a wood one that is so rigid it might cause the glass to break when it is fastened into the frame.

SOLID SUPPORTS FOR STRETCHING

Plywood Plywood provides an excellent support for small pieces of needlework or fabric that are difficult to stretch. It is also commonly used when framing three-dimensional items which must be screwed or otherwise attached to a sturdy backing, and for this purpose it is often covered with cloth. However, a large piece of plywood makes the picture so heavy that special measures must be taken to hang it, so whenever possible, pieces over 16" x 20" should be stretched on a lightweight backing.

Mounting Board Pieces of fabric or needlework smaller than 16" x 20" can be stretched on a mounting board such as Upson board, heavy chipboard, or Fome-Cor. Fome-Cor is superior for this purpose because its surface is acid-free and it is soft enough so that any knots in the back of the needlework may be pressed into the backing. Any of these boards will bend if a lot of pressure is applied at the corners, so if you have a tough stretching job, or if you are stretching something fairly large, you may want to strengthen the mounting board by using a piece of 1/8" plywood behind it. Simply attach the plywood to the back of the mounting board with double-stick tape before you begin stretching. When you stretch the fabric, you can staple the edges into the back of the plywood.

WOOD STRETCHER FRAMES A wood stretcher frame provides a strong, lightweight support for items of all sizes. The stretchers are about 3/4" deep, so if you use them, your selection of frames will be limited to those deep enough to cover the edge of the stretched piece.

You can assemble a stretcher frame using precut stretcher strips in about 20 minutes, or you can buy some lumber and build your own stretcher frame in a couple of hours. There is very little difference in cost.

Precut stretcher strips are available at art supply stores and framing stores, or you can mail-order them from Charrette or Twin City. They come in selected lengths from 8" to 60", and are approximately 3/4" deep and 1 1/2" wide. Oversized stretcher strips are also manufactured in lengths from 50" to 84". They are about 1" deep by 2 1/2" wide. They may be hard to find in local stores, but can be mail-ordered from Charrette.

Precut stretcher strips have slots inside the corners so that small wood pieces, called keys, may be inserted to tighten the fabric after it is stretched. They also have a raised edge so that the fabric is not in contact with the front surface of the stretcher.

Precut stretcher strips can be easily and quickly assembled at home with a staple gun, but since they slip out of square easily, working with them can be very frustrating.

You can build your own stretcher frame exactly the size you need. The corners will be stronger than the corners of a frame assembled from precut strips, and they will not slip out of square. But there is no way to tighten the fabric after it is stretched.

125

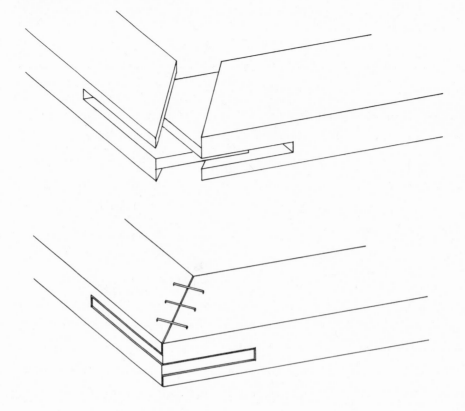

ASSEMBLING PRECUT STRETCHERS
TOOLS

> *Staple gun*
>
> *Carpenter's square or draftsman's triangle*

Set out the four pieces as they will go together.

Fit one corner together as tightly as it will go. Then check with a builder's square or draftsman's triangle to make sure that the outside of the corner is a right angle. Many stretcher bars are not perfectly cut, so the corner may not be meeting perfectly when held square. It is important for the corner to be a right angle even if it is not as tight as it could be.

Staple across the joint three or four times.

Turn the corner over and check for squareness again.

Staple it on the other side.

Repeat this procedure for the second corner.

Fit the fourth side into place and check both the remaining corners for squareness.

Staple both of the remaining corners.

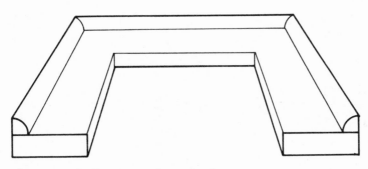

Stretcher frame with the outer edge raised.

TO MAKE A STRETCHER FRAME
TOOLS

Titebond glue	Backsaw
Hammer	Drill
Wire brads — 3/4"	Pliers
Wire brads — 2"	Nail set
Miter box	

The outer edge of a stretcher frame is raised so that the fabric is only in contact with the sides of the frame, not with the front surface. If the fabric were in contact with the front of the wood stretcher, any roughness or unevenness in the surface would show through. There are two common ways to build a strong homemade stretcher with a raised edge. You can use ordinary 1x2 lumber and add a strip of half-inch quarter-round molding to get a raised edge, or you can use Anderson Staff Bead, which is milled with a raised edge (in some parts of the country, this is called brick molding).

Attach the quarter-round to the 1x2 with a flat edge of the quarter-round lined up with the edge of the 1x2 as shown in the drawing. Glue the quarter-round in place with Titebond or any other strong wood glue, and nail it every 8" or 10" with ¾" wire brads.

Cut the stretcher strips with mitered corners. If it is difficult for you to remember which way the mitered cuts should go, each piece should appear as shown in the drawing below. To cut the strips, place the wood in the miter box as shown in the next drawing. Clamp it in place with a C-clamp or other clamp that will fit. Cut one end and

One side of a stretcher frame with mitered corners.

127

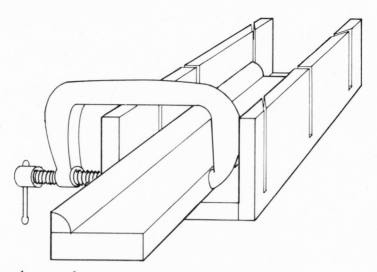

Clamping the stretcher strip into the miter box for cutting.

then measure along the outside edge of the stretcher strip to determine where the next cut should be.

Assemble the stretcher frame following the instructions for assembling a wooden frame in Chapter 20. Cross-nail each corner. You needn't putty the nail holes or corners — they won't show.

Seal the stretcher frame by painting it with polyurethane to help protect the fabric from the effects of acid in the wood.

Cross-brace the stretcher frame if necessary. A cross-brace spans the distance between two pieces of a stretcher frame to keep the frame from bowing inward when the fabric is stretched. Any length

Stretcher frames without and with a cross brace.

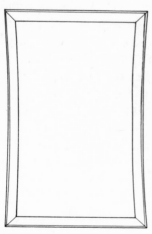
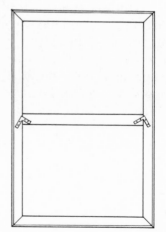

over 30″ should be braced. To determine the length of the brace, measure the distance between the two pieces near the end of the frame. Cut the brace, apply glue to both ends, and wedge it into place in the stretcher frame. Secure the brace to the stretcher frame with metal angles on both the front and the back. Place the angles slightly askew as shown; if they were lined up with the grain of the wood they could cause splitting.

PROCEDURE FOR STRETCHING FABRIC AND NEEDLEWORK Iron fabric to remove wrinkles or fold lines. Do not iron painted fabric, as the heat may affect the paint.

Block needlepoint or crewel embroidery.

Measure the fabric to determine the size of the stretcher frame or solid support.

Sew an extension strip onto the fabric if there is not enough border for stretching.

Build or assemble a stretcher frame or cut a solid support.

Cut an acid-free backing to use between fabric and a support which is acidic. If the support is wood, you may paint it with polyurethane instead so that the acids in the wood will not affect the fabric.

Stretch the fabric on the support.

Cleaning Needlepoint and Crewel Embroidery If the needlepoint or embroidery is dirty, it may be cleaned by hand washing in cold water with a mild soap such as Woolite. Squeeze it dry but do not wring it. Roll it in a dry towel to absorb excess moisture. While it is still damp, follow the instructions for blocking.

Blocking Needlework that is out of square *must* be blocked before it can be stretched successfully. Needlework that has not been blocked will not stretch smoothly, and you can't pull an out-of-square piece into position by just stretching it on a wood backing. The needlepoint canvas is likely to tear and needlepoint and crewel embroidery will pucker.

To block needlework you will need to make a blocking board. The best thing to use is a piece of soft fibrous board such as Homosote or Cellu-Tex; both absorb moisture and provide air for drying on both sides of the needlework. Plywood may be used, but as plywood does not absorb moisture the needlework will take much longer to dry.

Use a piece of heavy white fabric to cover the blocking board.

129

Stretch it around the board and staple or tack the edges in place on the back.

Draw a grid on the blocking board with a laundry marking pen. Be *very* sure it is indelible; try it first. Lines should be about 1" apart.

Lay the needlework on the blocking board and temporarily pin the four corners in place using the grid to help you position the corners.

Use push pins or thumbtacks to tack the center of one edge in place. Pull the needlework gently and tack the center of the opposite edge in place. Then tack the centers of the remaining two sides in place. *Never* put pins or tacks into the embroidered part of the cloth or canvas.

Work out toward the corners putting a few tacks or pins in one side then turning to the next side. Pull the fabric gently but do not try to stretch it.

Dampen the needlework with a damp cloth. Do not get it wet, but just moisten it evenly until it relaxes. Let it dry about 24 hours in a horizontal position.

Measuring the Fabric for Stretching   When you measure fabric remember that it will stretch, maybe a little, maybe a lot, and a design on a piece of fabric will be larger after it is stretched than before. To measure a piece of fabric accurately you must pull it tightly while you measure. This is easiest if you have a friend hold the fabric for you while you measure it. A fabric print with a border, or a painting with the edges clearly delineated, should be measured carefully because it may not actually be square. You should measure at both ends and in the middle for both dimensions. If there is some discrepancy, use the measurement that will most effectively set off the edges of the piece.

If you intend to frame the piece after you stretch it, the lip of the frame will cover ⅛" to ¼" on each side. Thus, if there is a pattern around the edge that should be visible after framing, add ¼" to ½" (depending on the lip of the frame) to each measurement.

Whenever possible the piece should be stretched on a rigid support and then measured to determine the frame size. But if you are stretching something to fit into an already assembled frame, remember that the thickness of the fabric will add ½₂" to ¼" to each dimension of the stretcher frame or support, and adjust your measurements accordingly.

You will need 1" to 3" of border on each side to pull around to the back of the support. If your backing is not very thick, you could

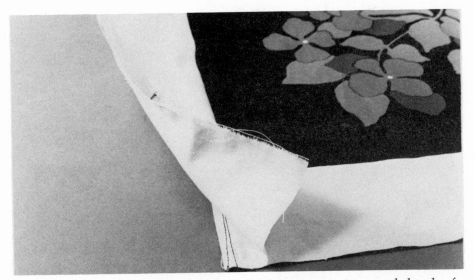

Sewing an extension strip on a piece of fabric to give it enough border for stretching.

do with less border, but it isn't easy. You can add an extension strip to the fabric if necessary.

Adding an Extension Strip to Fabric   If your piece of fabric doesn't have sufficient border for stretching, sew an extension strip of fabric along the edge. The fabric for the extension strip should be as similar as possible to the fabric you are stretching. Cut a strip about 3″ wide and about 2″ longer than the length of the side you want to extend. Place the right sides together and align one edge of the strip with the edge of the fabric. Sew the pieces together by hand or machine along a line about ½″ in from the edge. Iron the seam away from the center of the fabric.

Stretching the Fabric
> MATERIALS for Stretching Fabric on a Wood Support
>> *Thumbtacks, #3 or #4 screen tacks, or a staple gun
>>   and staples*
>> *Canvas pliers for stretching heavy fabric. (optional)*
> MATERIALS for Stretching Fabric on Fome-Cor or a Cardboard
Support
>> *Straight pins, push pins, or map tacks*
>> *Cloth tape, wide masking tape, or linen tape — Linen tape
>>   is acid-free and will hold longer than other tapes, but
>>   it takes longer to adhere.*

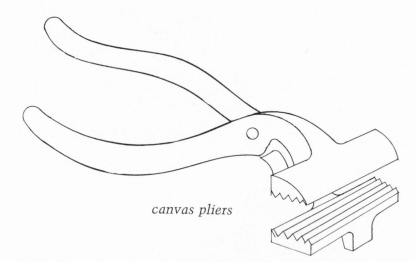

canvas pliers

When stretching fabric, work on all four sides at once, starting in the centers and working out to the corners. Temporarily secure the edges of the fabric to the back of the support using pins, tacks, or staples. Once the fabric is stretched into place, secure it permanently by setting the tacks or staples, replacing the pins with strong tape, or sewing the edges of the fabric in place. The latter method, called latching, is preferable to other methods since it is less likely to damage the fabric.

Place the fabric face-down on a clean surface.

Place the stretcher frame or support face-down on the fabric. If you are using a stretcher frame with a raised edge, the side with the

raised edge should be in contact with the fabric. If you have attached an acid-free paper or board to one side of the support, the acid-free surface should be against the fabric.

Position the support on the back of the fabric.

In the center of one side, pull the edge of the fabric around the support. Staple or tack into the back of a wood support. (Always place staples diagonally or they may tear the cloth.) Pin through the fabric into the edge of a cardboard or Fome-Cor support. Push the pins only partway into the support so they can be easily removed.

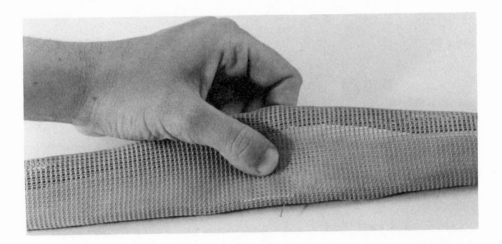

In the center of the opposite side, pull the fabric tight. Pin or staple it to the support.

Repeat for the other two sides.

Turn the piece over to see if the fabric is placed as you want it. If not, pull out the necessary pins, tacks, or staples and reposition it.

When the centers of all four sides are correctly placed, begin to work out toward the corners. On either side of the center, pull the fabric tight and secure it to the support. Turn to the next side and repeat. Continue around the piece, putting a couple of pins, staples, or tacks in each side. Pull the fabric toward the corners as you stretch it — this will make the corners easier to stretch into place when you get there. If the piece is rectangular rather than square, secure it twice on the long sides for every time you secure it on the short sides so that you will reach the corners from both directions at the same time.

As you stretch, turn the piece over occasionally and check to be sure the grain of the fabric or the straight lines in the design are really straight. If not, pull out the necessary staples, pins, or tacks and

133

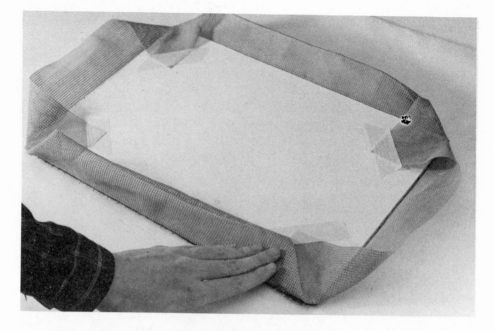

reposition the fabric. Secure the fabric as often as necessary to keep the threads straight — about every inch.

Fold the corners, then the sides, of the fabric around the support as shown.

Hammer tacks or staples tightly into place on a wood support or follow the instructions below for latching.

Tape the edges of the fabric down on a cardboard or Fome-Cor support. Use long strips of wide masking tape or cloth tape or small pieces of linen tape. To stick down the linen tape, moisten the shiny side and hold it in position for about 30 seconds. Then remove the

pins from the edge of the support. (If you are using Fome-Cor and straight pins, you can just push the pins all the way into the board and leave them there.)

Latching

MATERIALS

Pins or thumbtacks for positioning the fabric
Heavy duty thread — button or rug thread
Needle

Pin or tack the fabric to the edge of the support following the instructions for stretching given above. Inspect the piece from the front to make sure the lines of the fabric are straight. Be sure the pins or tacks are close enough together so that the fabric isn't sagging between them.

Place the piece face-down again, and using heavy-duty thread, sew in a zigzag pattern from one edge of the fabric to the other as shown. Make sure the needle catches the fabric as often as the pins or tacks that are holding it.

Repeat going in the other direction.

Latching

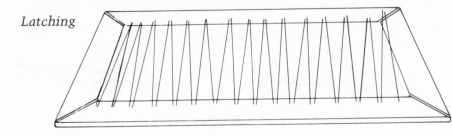

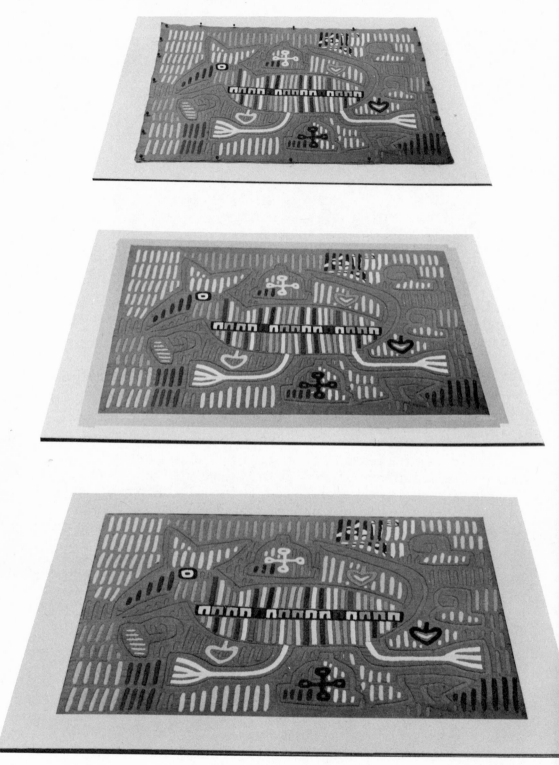

Special Directions for Stretching Very Fragile Items Very old or fragile cloth can't stand the stress of stretching and may be ruined by staples or tacks.

Stretch a piece of white muslin or linen on the support, following the instructions for stretching. Then very gently stretch the fragile piece of fabric on the cloth-covered support. Pin it to the backing cloth with straight pins to position it on the support. Fold the edges under so that the fabric won't ravel, and sew it to the backing cloth. Remove the pins.

Stretching a Piece of Fabric Flat on a Backing
MATERIALS
> *Push pins or map tacks*
> *Wide masking tape, cloth tape, or linen tape. The linen tape is acid-free and holds longer than the other tapes, but it takes longer to adhere.*

If a piece of needlework is to be matted and the outside dimensions of the mat are to be larger than the needlework itself, the least bulky way to stretch it will be to place it flat on a backing the same size as the outer dimensions of the mat.

You can stretch it on Fome-Cor, mounting board, or any other stiff backing.

Cut the backing about 2" larger than the mat is to be in each direction.

Place the fabric face-up on the backing.

Pin the centers of all four edges to the backing.

Work out toward the corners stretching the fabric gently and pinning it to the backing. Make sure the threads of the fabric are straight and the corners are square.

Tape the edges in place with strips of cloth tape, or masking tape, or small pieces of linen tape. To stick down the linen tape, moisten the shiny side and hold it in place for about 30 seconds.

Remove the pins.

Measure the fabric to determine the exact size of the mat.

Cut the mat.

Place the mat over the stretched fabric, position it as you want it, and trace the perimeter of the mat on the backing with pencil.

Remove the mat and trim the backing on the pencil lines.

Hinge the mat to the backing or attach it with double-stick tape.

17 Wood Moldings and Metal Stripping

YOU CAN BUY MOLDING already finished or you can buy it unfinished and apply stain, paint, or metal leaf yourself. Unfinished molding purchased at a lumberyard is generally the cheapest. However, the time required for finishing the wood yourself is considerable and it is a messy job requiring a ventilated work space. Unless you have had considerable experience with wood finishing, you will probably find it difficult to predict exactly what a particular finish is going to look like.

Both finished and unfinished moldings can be purchased at frame stores and at some art supply stores. Some custom frame shops offer only the service of custom framing and refuse to sell molding to individuals, so call before you go. Some lumberyards stock picture frame moldings and all have a selection of builder's moldings that can be combined to form picture frame molding. The selection will vary from one lumberyard to the next, so if you don't like what you see in one place, shop around. Of the raw moldings, fir and basswood are less expensive and are generally used when the molding is to have an opaque finish like paint or metal leaf. Hardwoods, such as walnut, birch, poplar, or mahogany, are more often finished with stains and clear finishes that bring out the natural beauty of the wood.

Some lumberyards will mill the wood to whatever profile you request. There is usually a fee for setting up the machinery in addition to the cost of the molding, and a minimum order of around 100 feet.

Another possibility is to start with a board and cut it the size and shape you want it. Unless you are experienced with woodworking tools, you will probably find this rather difficult. This is a wonderful way to use and display a beautiful piece of oak or walnut that you happen to find in your attic or garage. However, when you begin to shape your own molding, you should realize that it may not be exactly the same width at one end as it is at the other end, or the size of the lip may not be constant, or the wood you are working with may be warped — in other words, be as precise as you can when you cut the wood, but don't expect perfection. Minor discrepancies will not hinder the assembly of the frame.

Frame shops will sell you molding in long lengths or cut it to size for you. To cut the molding yourself, you will need a fine-toothed saw and a miter box. It may take a few tries before you can cut a professional-looking corner, so buy a little extra to practice on.

If you are going to cut the molding yourself and you need to figure out how much to buy, add the four dimensions of the artwork (with a mat if there is one) and then add eight times the width of the molding. This is because each time you cut a complete mitered corner, you waste a length of molding twice as long as the width.

COMBINING BUILDER'S MOLDINGS TO MAKE A PICTURE FRAME MOLDING Lumberyards stock wood moldings in a variety of shapes and sizes, some with lips and some without. It is easy to combine two or more of these moldings to get the shape you want for a frame. When you start to design your molding, remember that it must be deep enough to accommodate everything that will go into the frame. The depth of the frame, distance A, can

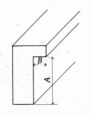

not be less than ¼" and still accommodate artwork, glass, mat, and backing. It will be easier to work with if it is at least ⅜" deep. It must be at least ¾" deep to cover the edge of a precut wood stretcher frame, deeper for a homemade one. The lip of the frame, distance B, should not be less than 3/16". A normal lip is 5/16" and it can be wider.

Some possible combinations are shown in the drawing. Each lumberyard will have its own selection of moldings, so see what's available to you and then design your molding accordingly.

To Combine Two Moldings Place a thin layer of glue on the smaller piece and place it on the other piece, lining up the edges.

Nail the two pieces together with wire brads about 10" apart. Set the brads just under the surface with the nail set and cover them with wood filler or gesso. If you plan to use a clear finish and don't want to have brads showing, clamp the pieces of molding together while the glue dries — about 24 hours — instead of using brads.

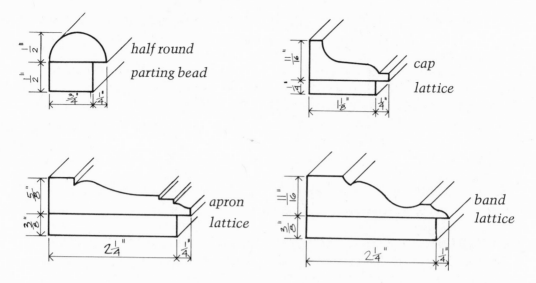

half round
parting bead

cap
lattice

apron
lattice

band
lattice

A few ways to combine builders' moldings to make picture frame moldings.

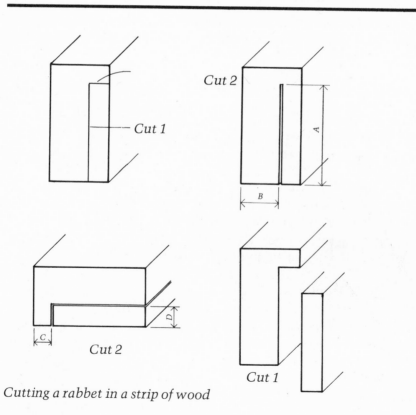

Cut 1

Cut 2

Cut 2

Cut 1

Cutting a rabbet in a strip of wood

Clean off all excess glue immediately. Any glue that dries on the surface will have to be removed by sanding.

CUTTING A RABBET IN A STRIP OF WOOD You can rabbet your own molding by making two quick cuts on a table saw. Draw the two cuts on the end of the molding.

First set the blade of the saw at height A. Set the guide at distance B from the blade. Make cut 1.

Then turn the wood with the top edge facing the guide. Set the blade at height D and the guide at distance C from the blade. Make cut 2.

Table saws are dangerous. Do not let your fingers get near the blade. When you get close to the end of a cut, push the wood the rest of the way through the saw with a long scrap of wood. Don't stand where the blade can throw wood chips and sawdust in your face.

MEASURING MOLDING The molding is always cut ⅛" longer than the glass, mat, and backing. This gives you enough clearance to drop the contents of the frame in from the back after the four corners are assembled, with enough room in the frame for the mat, artwork, and backing to expand and contract naturally without pushing against the side of the frame and buckling. It also leaves you a slight margin for error.

Measuring wood molding for cutting.

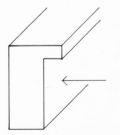

Standard wood molding

measure here for glass

measure here for backing

Double-lipped molding

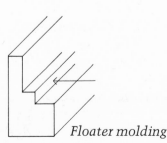

Floater molding

Stripping

Sometimes you will measure the artwork and find that the measurements are not consistent. Needlework and stretched canvas are especially difficult to measure since they tend to bulge at the corners. If in doubt cut the molding a little longer than you think you will need it. You can always trim a little if it's too large.

When you measure a molding for cutting, measure along the inner edge of the molding, the edge in contact with the artwork. See the drawing.

CUTTING THE MOLDING

TOOLS

    Tape measure or ruler
    Miter box
    Fine-toothed saw
    Small strip of wood to support the lip of the molding
    Clamp

If you are not accustomed to using a miter box, you may be confused as to which of the 45-degree cuts you should use for which end of the molding. Remember that each end of the molding will look like the drawing below after it is cut. The outside edge will be

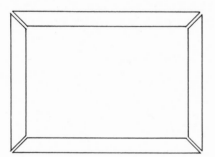
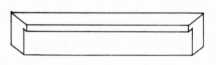

Strip of molding with mitered corners.

longer than the inside edge and the 45-degree cut will slant from the outside corner of the molding toward the center of the picture. If you need to, draw a picture of how the piece should look after it is cut and keep the drawing in front of you facing the same way as your molding while you position the molding in the miter box.

Before you cut the molding you should put a small strip of wood (balsa or basswood from a hobby store or an art supply store is perfect) under the lip of the molding to keep it from splitting as you cut. The strip of wood should not be as deep as the inside edge of the molding, and it should be wider than the rabbet so that when you clamp the

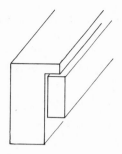

Strip of wood to keep the lip of the molding from splintering when it is cut.

molding into the miter box, the clamp rests on the wood strip instead of the molding.

Place one end of the stick of molding in the miter box, front-side-up, as shown.

Place the stick of balsa wood under the lip of the molding. It should be pushed tightly against the underside of the lip.

Clamp the molding in place in the miter box with a C-clamp or spring clamp. The clamp should press on the strip of wood under the lip of the molding rather than the molding itself, as the clamp can dent even hardwood molding. Clamp the molding as close as possible to the cutting line.

Make sure the bottom side of the molding is resting flat against the bottom of the miter box.

Clamping wood molding in the miter box for cutting.

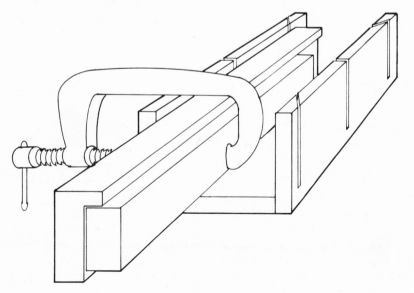

Place the saw in the groove and gently draw it toward you across the top of the molding to start the cut. Then continue to saw with light pressure. Whenever you exert too much pressure on the saw it will dig into the wood and stop. Make sure that you hold the saw vertical. If you tilt it to either side, the cut will be crooked.

Remove the molding from the miter box and measure along the inner edge to find the location of the next cut.

The cutting line will always be on the inner edge of the molding. To line up the molding accurately for the next cut, you must draw the line of the saw across the bottom of the miter box. (If your miter box is a wooden one, the saw has probably made its own line across the bottom already.) Each time you put the molding in the miter box, line up the cutting line with this line.

18 Buying Old Frames

ANTIQUE STORES, secondhand stores, or flea markets are excellent places to look for old frames, especially if you are interested in spending some time repairing and refinishing. But you should know what to look for.

Check the wood to see if it is sound. Check for soft spots or rotten spots in the wood. Dig your thumbnail into the back of the molding to see if the wood is firm or if it crumbles — crumbly or split wood may be a sign that the frame has been exposed to excess dryness. Holes or powdery areas in the molding may be evidence of insects.

Check to see if the corners of the frame are strong. When you exert pressure on the frame do the corners hold or are they loose? If you intend to cut the frame down, you should be able to cut a clean surface on each end of each stick of molding and build a strong corner. If you intend to leave the frame the size it is, the corner must be strong enough as it is or the wood at the corner must be sound enough to form a strong bond. If the wood is split at the corner or if so many nails have been put into it that there is little wood left, you will not be able to make a strong joint.

Evaluate the present finish on the frame. Do you like it the way it is or will you want to refinish it? How much refinishing will be necessary? If the finish is in good shape, a simple waxing may be all it needs. If the finish has been worn or damaged you may have to apply additional coats of finish or strip and refinish the whole frame.

If there is carved ornament on the frame, determine if it is actually carved wood or if it is gesso. Gesso is a white plasterlike material which is often used on frames to smooth the surface for painting or to simulate carved ornaments. Gesso can't stand rough treatment, and chips very easily, showing white where it is chipped. It is possible to find craftsmen who will take a mold from the carving remaining on a frame and make a new gesso ornament to replace the

145

missing part, but this is an ambitious project to try to complete successfully at home.

If the frame has veneer on it, check to see if the veneer is split, peeled, or blistered. If it is only lifting a little, it will not be too difficult to repair, but if there is extensive damage you may not be able to repair it yourself.

Notice how the corners of the frame are joined. An all-wood joint — dovetailed or splined — is stronger and more beautiful than a glued and nailed joint.

PREPARING OLD FRAMES FOR REFINISHING
Cleaning an Old Frame
MATERIALS

Butcher's Bowling Alley Wax
000 steel wool — a very fine-strand steel wool available at hardware stores for natural wood frames
A soft cloth for painted or gold leaf frames

Apply the Butcher's Wax with steel wool or a soft cloth using light pressure. The wax acts as a solvent for dirt and old polish. Go over the frame again with a clean cloth and more wax to remove the dirty wax. Then polish with a soft cloth.

Stripping a Frame By Scraping
MATERIALS

A steel scraper or a small piece of glass — about 2" by 3" (use single weight or double weight glass. Picture weight breaks too easily.) Cover all but one edge of the glass with masking tape.
Sandpaper — fine grit

If the surfaces of the frame are flat, you can scrape and sand to remove the old finish. This job is not nearly so awful as it is when you are removing the finish from furniture because frames are so small that it doesn't take very long. Hold the scraper at a 45-degree angle to the surface of the wood and scrape in the direction of the grain. Change the angle slightly from time to time as the edge wears down. Scrape until the finish is removed. Then sand with fine-grit sandpaper. I do not recommend using electric sanders on picture frames because they wear down delicate contours and sharp edges too easily.

Stripping a Frame with Chemicals
MATERIALS

Varnish brush

> *Denatured alcohol or a commercial paint and varnish re-*
> *   mover*
> *000 steel wool or brass-bristled brush*

If a frame has a complex contour or carving, a chemical remover will be the best way to remove the finish. Commercial paint and varnish remover is strong and fast-acting, but somewhat expensive; denatured alcohol costs less but takes longer to remove the finish. (*Stains* will not be completely removed from the wood by either method because they penetrate the wood; they can only be removed by sanding or bleaching.)

To remove finish with denatured alcohol, brush the alcohol onto the frame and then scrub the frame with very fine steel wool or a brass-bristled brush. Repeat as many times as necessary to remove the finish.

There are two kinds of commercial removers. Some you can wash off with water after you have stripped the frame; they will say so on the label. Others contain wax to enable the remover to penetrate the wood, and if all traces of the wax are not removed from the surface of the frame, later finishes will not dry properly.

To use a commercial remover, paint the remover onto the frame with a brush. Allow the finish to soften for a few minutes and then scrub off the finish with a brass brush or very fine steel wool. If the remover is not one that can be washed off with water, rub the frame down with benzene or denatured alcohol to remove any residue. Allow the frame to dry at least four hours before finishing.

19 Finishing Raw Wood

ALL FINISHING MATERIALS listed on the following pages can be acquired at a hardware store unless otherwise noted.

WOODS Softwoods are the evergreens such as pine and fir. They are cheaper than hardwoods and their grain and texture are usually less interesting, so softwoods are typically finished with opaque stains or paints, or with metal leaf.

Hardwoods are the deciduous trees — oak, walnut, maple, cherry, birch, mahogany, and poplar are some which are commonly used for frames. Hardwoods are usually finished with a clear finish or a transparent stain to enhance the grain, texture, and color of the natural wood. The term hardwood does not necessarily mean that the wood is hard. Maple is an extremely hard wood, but balsa wood (used for spacers in shadow box frames), one of the softest of all woods, is technically a hardwood. Basswood, a common wood for picture frame moldings, is a hardwood that looks very much like fir. Both basswood and balsa should be treated as softwoods for finishing purposes.

GENERAL INSTRUCTIONS Whenever you are applying a liquid finish to an already assembled frame, stick four or more thumbtacks into the back of the frame so that when you put it face-up on the table it will be elevated. This way the finish will not glue the frame to the work surface.

Purchase finish materials in small containers — it doesn't take much to cover a picture frame.

Wear rubber gloves. All finishing materials are hard on the hands.

Brushes used for finishing should be no wider than the molding.

Work in a well-ventilated area. Finishing materials give off noxious fumes.

Keep artwork away from finishing materials.

SANDING THE RAW WOOD
MATERIALS
Medium and fine grit sandpaper — Garnet paper and aluminum oxide paper are both good for sanding raw molding
A damp cloth or tack cloth for removing sawdust

Start with a medium grit paper and work up to a fine grit paper. Sand the surface of the wood until it is perfectly smooth and until any traces of previous finish have been removed. Sand with the grain of the wood. Wrap the sandpaper around a wood block if the molding is flat. Hold the sandpaper in your fingers to sand contoured or carved areas. After sanding, wipe the molding with a damp cloth or a tack cloth to remove the sawdust. Allow it to dry thoroughly before applying finish.

OIL FINISHES An oil finish penetrates the wood, darkening it slightly and bringing out the grain. Boiled linseed, Val-Oil, Stand oil, and Lemon oil are all satisfactory finishes for picture frames. Linseed Oil will darken more than others with the passage of time.

Apply the oil to the raw molding with a cloth. Wipe off the excess and allow it to dry overnight. Repeat once or twice.

After applying an oil finish, use a paste wax such as Butcher's Wax to protect the wood. Apply it with a soft cloth. Wipe off any excess and then buff it to a smooth gloss.

WAX FINISH Wax may be used as the final step over another finish or as the only finish on a wood molding. It protects the molding from scratches, stains, and waterspotting, and gives the finish a soft luster. Wax will darken the color of raw wood slightly but not as much as an oil finish. Use a paste wax as noted above.

STAINS Most of the stains available in hardware stores are penetrating oil stains. They soak into the wood, leaving a clear transparent look with the grain of the wood showing through clearly. Opaque oil stains are also available. They stain the wood, but instead of soaking into it, they stay on the surface, partially obscuring the grain and texture. Opaque stains are generally used for basswood, balsa, and softwoods.

Stores that carry stains usually have wood samples showing the color of the stain. If your molding is darker or lighter than the raw wood of the sample, it will also be a color different from the sample after staining. And if it is more open-grained or close-grained than the wood in the sample, it will take the stain differently and appear darker or lighter than the sample after staining.

149

To determine how a stain will look on your molding, stain a small patch on the back edge of the molding. Allow it to dry overnight and then apply one coat of the clear finish you intend to use. When this dries you will be able to see how the stain will look. If it is uneven or blotchy or too dark, or if it accentuates the grain too much, apply a thin coat of shellac (mix 1 part denatured alcohol to 2 parts shellac) to the raw molding before staining. This will partially seal the molding and let it stain more evenly and to a lighter shade.

If you can't decide between different stains, buy the lighter one. You can always apply a second coat.

To Apply Penetrating Oil Stain   Brush the stain on with a brush or rag. Brush in the direction of the grain. Allow it to stand for a couple of minutes, then wipe off the excess with a dry cloth.

Allow the stained wood to dry 48 hours before finishing.

Varnish or paint can't be applied over a penetrating oil stain since the stain will seep through the finish giving it a muddy appearance. Seal the surface of the stained wood with a thin coat of shellac before applying varnish.

Wax stains such as Minwax are penetrating oil stains with wax and a drying agent added. They stain the wood and give it a soft wax finish, and they dry much sooner than ordinary penetrating oil stains.

Varnish stains are a mixture of penetrating oil stain and varnish. They may give the wood a streaked appearance because they do not penetrate the wood well. They are also very slow-drying and collect dust as they dry. They are not very attractive or durable.

BLEACHES   Bleaches lighten the color of the wood. They are used primarily in refinishing. (Finish removers may lighten the color of stained wood slightly but they will not remove stain completely since the stain penetrates the wood.) Bleaches may also be used to lighten the natural color of the wood. They must be applied to the raw wood, so remove any previous finish before bleaching.

Wear rubber gloves when you work with bleaches; they are very caustic.

Bleaches are grain-raising, giving the wood a fuzzy appearance. To avoid this, brush water onto the raw wood, allow it to dry, and then sand down the raised grain before bleaching it.

There are many bleaching agents. Oxalic acid crystals are inexpensive and commonly available at hardware stores; you may use liquid laundry bleaches like Clorox. There are also commercial wood bleaches — these are usually more expensive but also stronger and more quick-acting than others.

To bleach the wood with oxalic acid crystals, dissolve ½ cup of the crystals in 1 quart of hot water. (Add the crystals to the water, not vice-versa). Use a glass or plastic container, not a metal one. Use a brush or sponge to apply the solution to the molding. Allow it to dry on the surface of the wood. Then brush off the dry crystals and check the color of the wood. If it isn't light enough, repeat the operation. When you finish, neutralize the surface of the wood by brushing on about an ounce of household ammonia diluted with a cup of water, or two ounces of Borax diluted with a cup of water. Do this in a well-ventilated area, and be sure you never mix Clorox and ammonia. The surface will blister if it isn't neutralized. Allow the wood to dry at least 24 hours before applying any finish.

To use laundry bleach on wood, dissolve an ounce of bleach in a cup of water. Brush it on the wood and when the wood is the color you want it, rinse it off with water. Neutralize the wood as described above and allow it to dry for at least 24 hours before applying any coats of finish.

If wood is placed in direct sunlight while the bleach is working, the bleaching will be hastened and intensified.

If you use a commercial wood bleach, follow the instructions on the container.

FILLER   Fillers are used after staining and before finishing to fill the pores of open-grained wood so that the finish will be smoother. They are not necessary, but some people prefer to use them. Open-grained woods commonly used for framing are oak, ash, mahogany, and walnut.

Close-grained woods — birch, basswood, cherry, maple, fir, pine, and poplar — require no filling, but the surface of the wood should be sealed with a wash coat of shellac to prevent subsequent coats of finish from soaking into the wood.

Fillers are clear or colored. Use the clear filler if you do not plan to stain the wood. Otherwise choose a filler to match the color of the stain. Fillers come in paste form and need to be thinned with turpentine. Follow the instructions on the container.

If you have used an oil stain on the molding, you must apply a wash coat of shellac (mix 1 part denatured alcohol with 2 parts shellac) to the surface before filling.

Brush the filler onto the wood with the grain and then across the grain. Let it stand for several minutes — until the surface turns dull. Rub off the excess filler, across the grain first, then with the grain. Lightly sand the surface when it is dry. Sand only with the grain of the wood.

151

METAL LEAF

MATERIALS

Metal leaf

Razor blade or gilder's knife

Gilder's tip — a wide flat brush with bristles about 2" long used to pick up the leaf and place it on the work. Gilder's tips are beautiful, but they cost about $12.00, so you probably won't want to get one unless you plan to do a lot of leafing. The purpose of the brush is to generate static electricity to pick up the leaf. A wide paintbrush with only a few rows of long soft bristles is a good substitute.

Quick drying gold size — This is the adhesive for the leaf. Be sure to get the quick drying size which is ready for leafing one to three hours after applying. The regular size takes 10 to 12 hours.

To Apply the Leaf   Paint the molding first if you wish — a base coat of color will slightly change the appearance of the leaf. Red, yellow, and olive green are all satisfactory colors to use under gold or bronze leaf. Black is normally used under silver or aluminum leaf.

Apply several coats of shellac to seal the wood (whether or not you have painted it). Allow each coat to dry and sand it lightly before applying the next coat. Make sure the last coat is perfectly smooth. Any scratches or brush marks will show through the leaf.

Apply an even coat of size to the molding.

Allow the size to dry until it is tacky. The instructions on the container will tell you how long.

Pick up a sheet of leaf with the gilder's tip and place it on the molding. If the molding is very small, you may want to cut the leaf into smaller pieces before applying it.

Press the leaf into place with the tip of the brush.

Continue applying leaf. Each sheet should overlap the previous one about ¼" at the edge. If you miss any spots, go back and fill in with a small piece of leaf. If any sheets have not adhered properly, go back and smooth them into place.

Allow the leaf to dry at least 8 hours.

Brush off any excess leaf and lightly rub the entire surface with a soft cloth.

Apply a coat of clear or orange shellac to seal the leaf from the air.

Antique if you wish.

SHELLAC Shellac is an alcohol-base finish. It dries dust-free in about fifteen minutes and is ready for a second coat in about two hours. It is commonly used as a sealer to prevent knots and streaks in the wood from bleeding through the finish and to seal oil stains. It is also used as a final finish, but it is not waterproof, so it should be protected with a coat of paste wax when it is so used. Shellac over six months old won't dry properly, so buy it in small containers and check the date on the can before buying it. It is thinned with denatured alcohol.

Shellac is white or orange. Use the white shellac as a sealer under a clear finish, or as a clear finish. You can use either one under an opaque finish. Use orange shellac over a gold leaf finish to give it a warm glow.

Several thin coats of shellac are better than one or two thick coats. Lightly sandpaper or steel wool each coat when it is dry.

VARNISH The most important consideration when buying varnish is to get one that is fast-drying, as varnish collects dust while it dries. Synthetic resin varnishes such as polyurethane are fast-drying, and they are fine for picture frames. You don't have to be concerned about the toughness or durability of the varnish, as a picture frame isn't going to get that much wear. Varnishes come with matte, semigloss, and glossy finish, so be sure to get the one you want.

Varnish gives the wood a clear, water-resistant finish. It can be rubbed to produce a very smooth surface.

PAINTING A RAW WOOD MOLDING It doesn't take a lot of paint to paint a picture frame. If the color you want is a custom-mixed one, you will spend a lot of money and have a lot of paint left over if you buy it at a hardware store or paint store. Instead, shop at hobby stores for the enamels used on model airplanes and for the many new products for decoupage and other crafts. There is a wide assortment of matte finish, glossy finish, spray or brush-on, water base paints in small containers. You must use a sealer or primer on the raw wood so that the pattern of the grain will not show through. Read the instructions on the container to determine which sealer or primer to use with the paint.

Acrylic artists' paints can also be used on frames. Prepare the wood by sanding and then brushing on a thin layer of gesso. (Thin it with water to the consistency of cream.) Brush marks show if the paint is too thick, so thin it with water and put on several coats. They dry quickly. If acrylic paint dries on your brush, use denatured alcohol to remove it.

153

If you are painting over an earlier finish, sand or steel wool it lightly so that the paint will hold. If the previous finish is an oil-base stain, seal it with a thin coat of shellac before painting over it.

ANTIQUING An antiquing glaze may be applied over a stained, painted, or metal leafed finish. You can buy an antiquing kit which contains a base paint and a glaze, or you can mix your own glaze.

To make an oil base antiquing glaze, mix 1 part boiled linseed oil and 3 parts turpentine with a little bit of oil paint pigment to make the glaze the color you want it.

Seal stained surfaces or metal leaf with a wash coat of shellac.

Apply the glaze with a brush or cloth. Allow it to set up for a few minutes. Then wipe it off with a cheesecloth or brush. Allow the glaze to remain in the corners and crevices to simulate actual wear. A cloth and a brush will give different effects, and you can use a circular or a straight motion for different patterns.

Apply a coat of varnish as a protective finish (optional).

To Antique Acrylic or Latex To make an antiquing glaze for acrylic or latex paint, mix 1 part acrylic paint (burnt umber and raw sienna are commonly used) with 4 parts acrylic matte medium or gel medium (the gel medium will produce a shiny finish, the matte medium, a flat one).

Brush the glaze onto the frame and immediately wipe it off with a dry rag, leaving it in the corners and crevices.

No protective finish is necessary.

Other Methods of Antiquing You can also use rottenstone powder to produce an antique effect. Lightly dust the powder onto the surface of the frame while the final finish is still tacky, but not while it is still wet. This will give the molding a dusty, speckled appearance.

A similar effect can be achieved by spattering the surface with black paint. Use oil paint over an oil finish, acrylic paint over an acrylic one. Dip a toothbrush into the paint and rub it over a small piece of screen to spatter the paint.

If you plan to use either of these techniques, you should experiment with the medium first to find out what effects are possible.

RUBBING A FINISHED SURFACE
MATERIALS
Pumice stone and/or rottenstone
Cheesecloth or a felt pad
Water or oil as a lubricant

Two or three soft clean cloths to clean the surface

A gloss finish — varnish, shellac, lacquer, or enamel — may be rubbed to the desired shine and smoothness. Powdered pumice stone and rottenstone are the rubbing agents commonly used. They are abrasives and work the same way on a finished surface that sandpaper works on raw wood. The finer the powdered stone and the longer you rub, the smoother and more polished the surface will be.

Pumice stone, the coarser of the two, is used to rub down bumps, bubbles, or other imperfections in the finish and to give the piece a matte finish.

Rottenstone, the finer abrasive, is then used to bring up the shine.

A surface to be rubbed should first be given several coats of finish — two or three more coats than you would normally give it. This is especially important for moldings with ridges or raised areas since the abrasive rubs through the finish easily and raised surfaces receive more rubbing.

Oil can be used as a lubricant on any finish, but it leaves a film on the surface that must be removed with turpentine or paint thinner. Water can be used as a lubricant on any finish except shellac. It is easy to clean the surface with water after rubbing, but the rubbing compound cuts through the finish much more rapidly with water lubricant than it does with oil. Therefore water requires less rubbing, but also makes it easy to rub through the finish.

Instructions for Rubbing Dip the cheesecloth or felt pad in a dish of water or oil and then in the powdered stone. Rub it lightly on the surface of the molding in the direction of the grain. Avoid rubbing ridges or raised areas too much.

Dip a clean cloth in the lubricant and remove the powdered stone from the molding surface.

Wipe the surface clean with a dry cloth.

If necessary repeat the rubbing or change to a finer abrasive to get a higher shine.

20 Joining the Corners of a Wood Frame

THE CORNERS OF A wood frame are joined with glue and brads. The glue is actually the strongest part of the joint once it sets up, but it takes about 45 minutes in the vise before the glue alone is strong enough to hold the corner. (The glue takes several hours to set up to its full strength.) Brads are used to hold the corner while the glue is setting and to give added strength to the finished corner. The vise holds the corner in place while you are nailing and gluing.

TOOLS

Vise or corner clamps
Titebond or other strong wood glue
Hammer
Hand drill
Nail set
Needlenose pliers with wire cutter
Wire brads — about as long as the molding is wide
Small wood sticks or mat scraps for applying glue
More small wood sticks or mat scraps to cushion the molding against the vise.
Putty or wax crayon the same color as the finished molding
Tissues to wipe off excess glue and putty.

The first step is to check to make sure that the frame is the right size. Lay the four frame pieces around the picture, glass, and backing, and, holding the corners together, check the length of each side. The frame should fit loosely so that after you have joined all four corners you will be able to drop the picture in from the back (the only exception to this is the floater frame, which accepts the artwork from the front — tolerances are the same). The frame should not be so large that the edge of the picture or glass will show after the frame is assembled. If the frame is too large, trim the pieces before going any further.

At this point make a mental note whether your frame is horizontal or vertical since you will need to know later. If the frame is

Trying the molding around the artwork to make sure it is the right size.

square or close to square, mark on the back of each piece "side," "top," or "bottom."

Remove the artwork from your work area and put it in a safe place where it can't get scratched or damaged by glue or putty.

Leave the four frame pieces laid out in a rectangle just as they were before you removed the picture. Leave the pieces in position whenever you are not working with them as a safeguard against switching two pieces around and gluing the wrong ends together.

Check your vise and clean off any dried glue that has collected on the top surface, the bed of the vise, where you are going to put the molding. Remove it by scraping with a screwdriver — if it is not removed it will lift the molding up and the corner will not meet properly.

FIRST CORNER Place one corner of the frame in the vise, one piece at a time. The molding should be face-up in the vise. If you put it in any other way it may be scratched. When you tighten the vise place a small Popsicle-stick or strip of mat board between the vise and the outside edge of the frame. Don't worry, for now, about whether the corner meets; just clamp the two pieces in the vise.

Move the molding pieces forward one at a time until they meet.

157

Placing the frame pieces in the vise.

(Don't try to move both pieces at once because it is too easy to drop one.) The entire seam should meet along the front face of the molding and down the edge. If the corner meets at the top edge and gaps at the bottom, the two pieces probably need to be pushed closer together. The molding tends to lean inward in the vise so that the top edge meets before the bottom of the seam. Pull the top edge of the molding outward a little and push the two pieces closer together. If the bottom meets but the corner gapes at the top, see if the molding is sitting flat on the bed of the vise — it should not be raised. If that isn't the problem, the molding may be cut crookedly. Sometimes you can compensate by lifting one end of the molding or twisting it slightly to close the gap. The slight distortion that this causes is only

Corner gaping at the bottom.

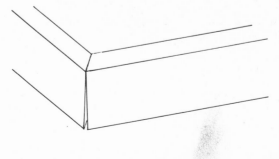

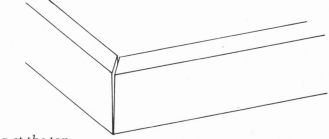

Corner gaping at the top.

a problem if you are building a small frame with a wide molding.

If you can't get the pieces to meet properly, remove them from the vise and set up the corner again on a flat tabletop. Determine which piece is cut badly and sand or trim it until the corner meets properly. (Any piece that is trimmed should be tested around the artwork again to make sure it still fits.)

Gluing the Corner Once you have set up the corner in the vise, remove one piece and apply glue to both faces of the joint, just enough so that a little squeezes out when you replace the corner in the vise. Put the molding back in the vise, and wipe off the excess glue. Since the corner has already been set up, it should fit; but if

Applying glue to the corner.

159

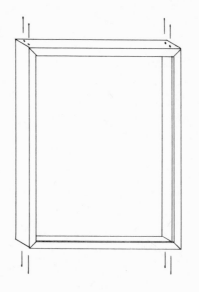

Put the brads into the frame from the top and bottom.

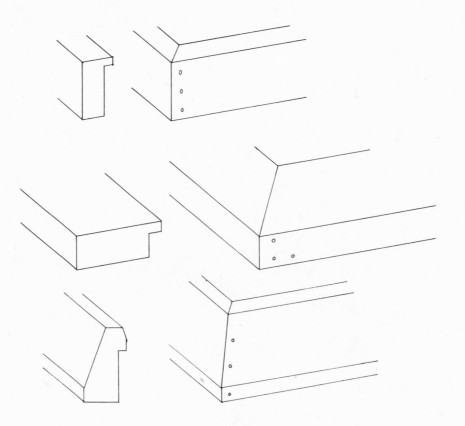

necessary, readjust the corner until it meets perfectly. Make sure the two pieces are pressed tightly against each other.

Clean off all the excess glue now, using a damp napkin. Glue is more difficult to remove after it dries on the surface of the frame. Since the corner is held tightly in the vise you can proceed with the next steps without waiting for the glue to dry.

Nailing the Corner   Wire brads are used for assembling frames because they have almost no head. The brad should be approximately as long as the molding is wide. Size is not crucial, but it is better to have it a little long than too short.

The brads may be put into the frame from the top and bottom of the picture to make them less easily seen; this is an aesthetic decision, not a structural one, and if you prefer, you can put the brads in from the side of the frame. There should be at least two brads in each corner of even the thinnest molding for stability so that the joint can't pivot. Larger moldings will need three brads in each corner, and

Where to put the brads.

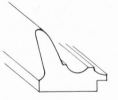
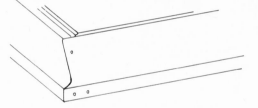
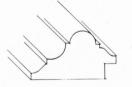

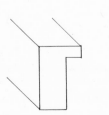

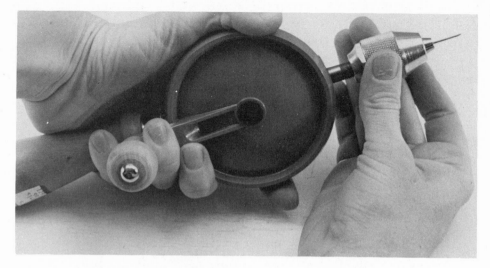

Loosening the drill to put the brad in.

if the frame is very large — over 24″ x 30″ — it is best for added strength to cross-nail the corner, putting two brads in from the top and bottom and one or two brads in from the side in each corner.

The shape of the molding will determine exactly where you put the brads. If you put the brad too far away from the corner, it will miss the other molding and protrude into the inside corner of the

Drilling holes for the brads in the corner of the frame.

frame. On the other hand if you put the brad too close to the corner, the joint will be weak and the wood may split. You want to place the brad so that it goes into the center of the other molding.

Drill holes for the brads — if you drill first, you are less likely to split the wood, crack the finish, bend the nail, or put it in crooked. You don't need to purchase drill bits: you can use a brad the same size as those to be used in the frame. Clip the head off with wire cutters or the wire cutting section of a pair of pliers to keep the brad from wobbling in the drill. Next insert the brad in the drill. To do this, hold the handle still and turn the chuck to open and close the mouth of the drill. When you drill the holes, do not let the drill chuck touch the frame and scratch it.

Tap the brads with the hammer as far as you can without hitting the molding. There is no need to hit them hard, but you should hold the molding so that it won't slide in the vise.

Use a nail set to tap the brads in further — until the heads are just below the surface of the wood.

Fill the nail holes and any cracks or chips in the corner with putty. Use a flat toothpick to press a dab of putty into the nail hole. If you are using a child's wax crayon for putty, hold it over a flame for a couple of seconds to soften it before pressing it into the nail holes.

Setting the brads with a nail set and tackhammer.

Two corners of the frame joined correctly.

Two corners of the same frame joined incorrectly.

164 Supporting the rest of the frame while one corner is in the vise.

Wax putty should be used only on already finished molding or on raw molding that will not have a finish, since wax clogs the pores of the wood and does not allow the finish to penetrate. If you intend to paint or metal leaf the frame after it is assembled, you can fill the nail holes and corners with gesso or wood filler. If you intend to apply stain, paste wax, varnish, or other clear finishes after assembling the frame, don't use any putty until after finishing; even a clear finish will alter the color of the wood slightly, so it's much easier to match the color of the finish if you putty afterward.

Wipe off all excess putty until the corner is clean.

Leave the corner in the vise for at least five minutes after you finish working on it. When you do remove the corner from the vise, it will still be fragile, so carefully clean out any glue that has squeezed out inside the corner and set the corner aside. As you loosen the vise to remove the molding, place one hand on top of the frame to make sure it doesn't fall.

SECOND CORNER Join the opposite corner of the frame next. This corner will look exactly like the first one with the long and short pieces in the same place. If you switch the two pieces around and glue the wrong ends together, this is the way your frame will look. If you make this mistake, take apart the corner that you glued last by holding both sticks of molding near the corner and gently working them apart. Then pull the brads out with pliers.

COMPLETING THE FRAME Join the third and fourth corner just as you did the first two. You will probably find it necessary to place something under the pieces of molding opposite the corner you are working on so that the frame won't sag and place stress on the corners you have just glued.

When you join the fourth corner, put glue into the corner before putting it into the vise. The rest of the steps are the same as they were for the first three corners.

21 Fitting Art into a Wood Frame

FITTING INCLUDES ASSEMBLING all the contents of the frame, placing them in the frame, fastening them in, and sealing the back. Four methods of fitting are described here; check to see which one applies to your frame.

First is the standard method for fitting when you have artwork with mat, glass, and backing. It can be followed even if you don't have all of these components.

The second method is for frames with spacers that separate the glass from the artwork; shadow box frames; and frames with mats, glass, and backing where the glass is to be dust-sealed.

The third is for fabric or other artwork on a wood support or stretcher frame and for rigid items such as sand castings and mosaics.

The fourth method is for any artwork that will be viewed from two sides.

METHOD ONE — STANDARD FITTING PROCEDURE

Use this method for fitting artwork with mat, glass, and/or backing. Use it also for dry mounted or wet mounted artwork with or without glass, and for fabric stretched on a support other than wood, with or without glass.

Assemble all the parts in order (generally stiff backing, protective backings, artwork, mat, glass) face-up on the table. Of course you may have all of these components or only a few of them.

Make sure that the glass is clean and free of lint or dust, the mat is not smudged or fingerprinted, and there are no hairs or other foreign objects under the glass. Line up all the edges exactly.

Place the frame face-up on top of everything else. It should fit easily into place. If it doesn't, check the inside corners of the frame. A nail protruding into the corner or excess glue gathered there may be in the way.

If the artwork has raised areas, be sure the glass isn't resting on them, as they may crack it. If this is a problem, follow Method Two and use spacers.

Reach under the frame with both hands and lift the contents of the frame into place against the lip. Turn the whole frame over and place it face-down on the table. Make sure that mat, glass, and backing fit loosely in the frame. If the mat or backing is too tight take it out and trim it with a sharp mat knife and a metal ruler, or it may warp or ripple. If the glass is too tight it won't go into place against the lip of the frame. It is difficult to trim small bits from the edge of glass, so if the discrepancy is small try sanding the edge of the glass with emery cloth or shaving the inside edge of the frame with a mat knife. If any of the pieces are too loose, their edges will be visible from the front of the frame. Anything that is too loose must be cut again.

Do not slide the frame on the table when it is face-down; the finish may scratch easily.

Turn to page 168 and follow the instructions for fastening the artwork into the frame.

METHOD TWO — FITTING WITH SPACERS AND/OR DUST-SEALING Follow these steps if you are using spacers to separate glass from the artwork, if you are building a shadow box frame, or if you are dust-sealing the glass.

Place the frame face-down on the table.

Place the glass in the frame from the back. To do this, lift one edge of the glass, leaving the opposite edge to rest on the table. Pick up the glass by the top edge only and place the bottom edge in position against the lip of the frame. Lower the glass into position in the frame, reaching under the frame to support the glass with the other hand when you release the edge.

Dust-Seal the Glass   (This step is optional.) Dust-sealing is done by fastening the glass into the frame with masking tape before putting in the rest of the contents. It is advantageous both because it seals out dust from the front of the frame and because it cushions the glass and makes it less likely to break when the frame is jarred — obviously a good measure for pieces that will be moved often or shipped a long distance.

Cut a strip of masking tape as long as one side of the glass and lay its edge just over the edge of the glass, not far enough to be visible from the front of the frame. Press the tape into the crack between the edge of the glass and the frame, and smooth the rest of the tape in place along the inside of the molding.

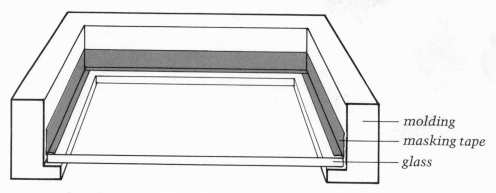

molding
masking tape
glass

Dust-Sealing the glass.

You may dust-seal the glass and then put spacers in the frame according to the next set of instructions, or you may dust-seal the glass and put your artwork with mat and/or backing into the frame, skipping the instructions for spacers.

Placing Spacers in the Frame   Spacers may be very thin strips of mat board or rag board if minimal separation is needed between glass and artwork, or they may be balsa wood strips as thick as necessary to accommodate three-dimensional artwork. The inside edges of the spacers will be visible from the front, so choose spacers that will be compatible with the frame. Balsa wood spacers can be painted, stained, or covered with fabric.

Cut two spacers exactly the same length as the inside edge of the frame. (Spacers do not need to be cut with mitered corners, as the corners will not be visible.) Spread a thin layer of glue on the backs of the spacers and glue them into place on the inside of the molding; they should fit snugly against the glass. Clean off any excess glue immediately. Clamp the spacers in place or hold them for 5 to 10 minutes so that the glue can begin to set. Then measure the other two sides of the frame and cut spacers to fit between the two already inserted. Glue them into place.

Check the inside surface of the glass once more to make sure it is free of fingerprints, glue, and dust.

Place the artwork and backings in the frame. Then, holding the contents in place with both hands, turn the frame over and check once more for lint or dust under the glass.

FASTENING THE ARTWORK INTO THE FRAME Lay the frame face-down on the table with the contents in place. In most frames the surface of the backing will be below the back edge of the molding, but if the backing is level or nearly level with the molding,

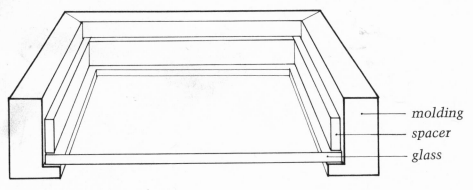

Putting spacers into a frame.

remove the backing, place it flat on the table, and rub the head of a hammer along all four edges to flatten them. Then replace the backing in the frame.

Use wire brads to fasten the contents into the frame. If the molding is ½″ wide or less, use a ⅝″ wire brad. For a larger frame, use ¾″, ⅞″, or 1″ wire brads depending on what you have handy. The brads may slip sideways a little and go crookedly into the frame, but they should not stick out from the back of the frame — they will puncture the dust seal and scratch your wall. If you have glass in the frame don't lean or press on the backing. The glass is easily broken.

There are fitting tools made specifically for placing the brads. They are not widely available and are costly enough so that it doesn't make sense to buy one unless you plan to frame a great many pictures. Instead of a fitting tool you may use a pair of pliers, a nail set, or a tack hammer to push the brads into place.

Fitting With a Fitting Tool   Place the nail flat on the backing. Hold it in place with your finger and gently squeeze it into the molding with the fitting tool. Push the brad far enough into the frame so that it doesn't wobble, but not all the way through the frame. When you have placed one brad correctly, set the fitting tool by loosening the wing nut on the shaft, placing the lower jaw on the outside edge of the frame and setting the upper jaw so that it rests on the head of the brad when the tool is squeezed shut.

Fitting With a Nail Set   Hold the nail set with your fingers wrapped around the pointed end, and the blunt end sticking out toward your thumb. Hold the brad in place on the back of the picture. Hook your thumb around the outside edge of the molding and press the nail into place with the side of the nail set. This is rather clumsy at first but

169

Fastening the brads into the back of the frame with a fitting tool.

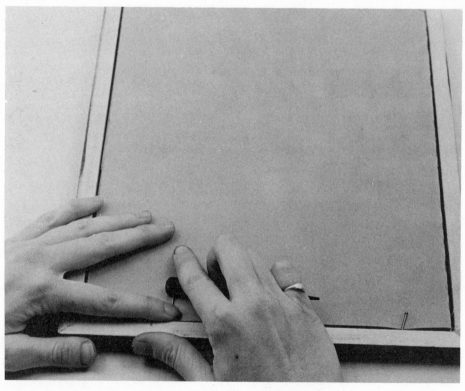

Fastening brads into the back of the frame with a nail set.

you can become proficient at it with practice. It works much better on softwood moldings than on hardwood.

Fitting With a Pair of Pliers   If your frame is fairly thin, you can drive the brads in with a pair of pliers (not the needlenose type). Use a wad of cotton or cloth or a folded piece of paper to pad the outside of the frame. Hold the nail in place on the backing with one hand. Open the pliers and place one jaw on the outside edge of the frame with the padding in place, and the other jaw on the head of the brad. Slowly squeeze the pliers together to drive the brad into the molding. (The brad should only be driven in partway — it is easy to push it all the way through if you aren't careful.)

Fitting With a Tack Hammer   If you do not have glass in your frame, you can use a tack hammer to put the brads in. Hold the nail in place on the backing. Rest the head of the hammer on the backing in the frame and without lifting it, gently tack the brad into place. This is not a good method to use when you have glass in the frame, since it jars the frame and the glass can easily break.

Fastening brads into the back of the frame with pliers.

Once you have placed all the brads, use the blunt end of the nail set to press down any that are sticking out from the backing.

Sealing the Back of the Frame   The crack between the backing and the molding must be sealed so that dust and insects can't enter by the back of the frame. If the backing is flush with the back of the molding, place a wide strip of masking tape across the crack at the edge of the backing and trim off the ends of the tape just inside the edges of the frame.

If the backing is recessed in the frame, place the tape first along the back of the molding with most of it extending over the back of the frame. Then trim the ends just inside the edge of the molding with a mat knife and press the tape all the way into the corner to seal the picture.

Brown paper is often used as a seal on the back of frames. This works until the paper is torn; then you no longer have a seal. Tape doesn't tear nearly so easily, and should be used as a seal first — brown paper can then be glued over the back of the frame, if desired, for looks. To apply brown paper to the back of the frame, spread a thin layer of glue along the back of the molding. With a moist sponge dampen a piece of brown paper, a little larger than the frame, and press it into place. When you are sure it will hold, trim off the edges with a mat knife about 1/8" in from the edge of the frame.

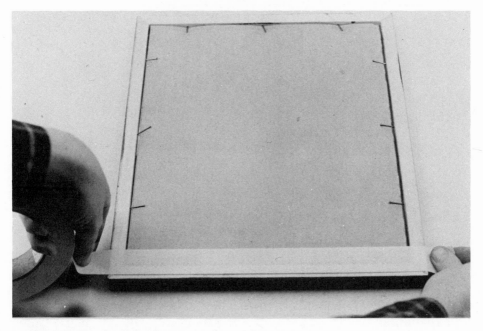

Sealing the back of the frame with masking tape.

METHOD THREE — FITTING FOR ARTWORK ON A WOOD SUPPORT Use this method if you are framing artwork stretched on a wood support or mounted on a wood backing, and for other rigid items like sand castings and mosaics.

The lip of a wooden frame is abrasive to a painted surface, so if you are framing a painting, you may want to pad the underside of the lip with felt. Felt with an adhesive backing is available at dimestores or hardware stores. Cut it in very thin strips (thinner than the lip of the frame) and stick it to the underside of the lip so that it doesn't show from the front of the frame. If you use regular felt and glue it in place, use only the minimal amount of glue; dried glue can also be abrasive.

If you are framing a piece of stretched fabric, a batik, or a piece of silk that is particularly valuable or fragile, you may want to cover the

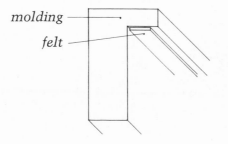

metal strip *offset clip* *turn button*

Metal fasteners for fitting.

entire inside edge of the frame with felt to keep wood splinters from catching the threads.

TOOLS

Screwdriver

Metal mending strips, offset clips, or turn buttons

Screws

Lay the artwork face-up on a table. Put the frame face-up on top of it and gently slip it into place. If the artwork does not go in easily, place the frame face-down on the table and try putting the artwork in from the back. The stretcher should be loose in the frame, with room to expand and contract normally. If it is fitting tightly in the frame, carve out the inside of the molding with a chisel or a mat knife.

Metal Strips If the back edge of the stretcher is level or almost level with the back of the frame, use metal strips, purchased at a hardware store, to hold it in. Screw one end of the strip into the back of the molding with the other end extending over the back of the stretcher. Do not screw it into the stretcher bar; this could cause splitting when the wood in stretcher and frame expands or contracts. Metal strips can easily be moved aside to remove the painting. Another version of the metal strip, called a turn button, is available through picture frame suppliers.

Fastening artwork on canvas into a wood frame with a metal strip.

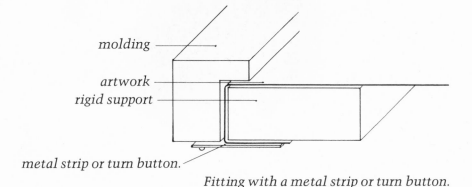

molding

artwork
rigid support

metal strip or turn button.

Fitting with a metal strip or turn button.

Offset Clips or Mirror Clips   If the back edge of the stretcher sits below the back of the frame or extends beyond it, you can bend the metal strips or use bent metal pieces called offset clips or mirror clips to hold the picture in. These screw into the back of the molding.

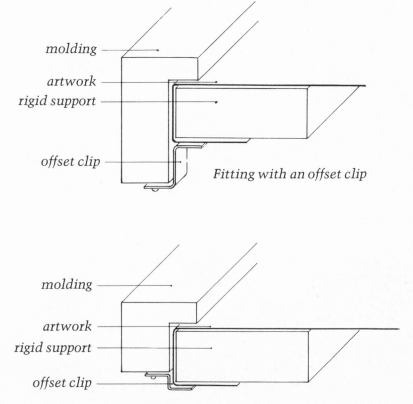

molding

artwork
rigid support

offset clip

Fitting with an offset clip

molding

artwork
rigid support

offset clip

Fitting with an offset clip

175

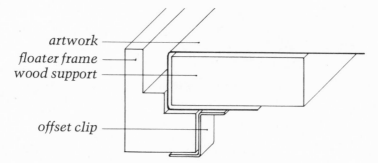

Fitting artwork into a floater frame with offset clips.

Fitting Artwork on Wooden Stretchers into a Floater Frame   Place the floater frame face-up on the table.

Place the artwork in the frame from the front.

Turn it over and use offset clips or mirror clips to hold the artwork in place. Screw the clips into the back of the wooden stretcher and place them so that the clips extend around the back of the molding.

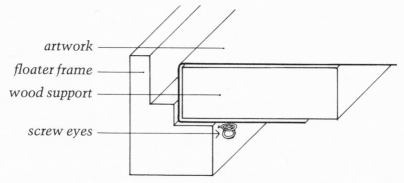

Fitting artwork into a floater frame with screw eyes.

An alternative arrangement if you have no mirror clips available is to use several screw eyes to hold the picture in. Place one screw eye in the inside edge of the molding just behind the artwork. Then stick the second screw eye through the first one and screw it into the back of the stretcher. You have to put all the screw eyes into the molding before you can begin putting the other screw eyes into the back of the stretcher.

Sealing the Back of the Frame   Tack or staple a piece of cardboard or Fome-Cor to the back of the stretcher to keep out dust and to keep the artwork from being punctured from behind. This is not necessary if the support is a solid piece of wood.

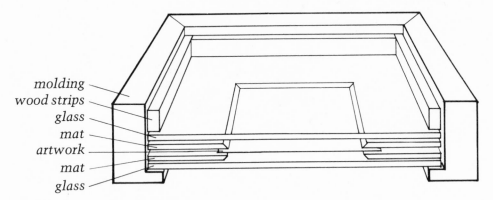

molding
wood strips
glass
mat
artwork
mat
glass

Fitting for a two sided frame.

METHOD FOUR — TWO-SIDED FRAMES   Use this method for a two-sided frame or framing a stained-glass window or other object to be viewed from both sides.

Finish the back of the molding.

Put the frame face-down on the table.

Place the artwork in the frame from the back.

Measure the distance from the back surface of the artwork to the back of the molding. Cut wood strips this width by about ¼". These can be balsa or basswood.

Finish the wood strips.

Cut two wood strips the same length as the opening in the back of the frame. Put them in place and tack through them into the inside edge of the molding with ½" wire brads.

Cut two more wood strips to fit between the two you have already put in. Tack them in place.

177

Assembling Frames

Note

The following chapters contain instructions for assembling a variety of frames. Chapter numbers in parentheses refer to the chapters in Part Two where you will find the material or technique described in detail. You may or may not be using all the components described, so instructions that don't apply to your frame may be omitted.

The procedure for preparing the contents of the frame is the same for most frames, and is therefore outlined below; the instructions for the specific frame you are building will describe any variations.

FABRIC OR NEEDLEWORK Prepare the contents of the frame as follows:

Iron the fabric to remove fold lines or wrinkles. Do not iron painted fabric, as heat may affect the paint.

Block and press needlepoint or embroidery. (Chapter 16)

Stretch the artwork on a rigid backing. (Chapter 16)

Measure the stretched piece. (Chapter 10)

Cut the mat if you are using one, and try it around the artwork to be sure it fits. (Chapter 11)

Cut and clean the glass or acrylic if you are using it (Chapter 12).

Cut a stiff backing to put into the frame behind the stretched artwork. (This backing is optional — when used it keeps brads from pulling or tearing the cloth during fitting and keeps fabric on stretcher frames from being punctured from behind and gives the back of the frame a more finished appearance.)

ARTWORK ON PAPER Prepare the contents of the frame as follows:

Clean or flatten the artwork if necessary. (Chapter 9)

Measure the artwork. (Chapter 10)

Cut the mat if you are using one and try it on the artwork to be sure it fits (Chapter 11). If you plan to paint the mat or cover it with fabric, do this first. The width of the fabric may add a little to the measurements of the mat, so remeasure it before cutting the glass or backing; and since it's hard to visualize how a painted mat will look, you may want to cut the outside of the mat a little large and then trim it to the proper size after decorating it and seeing it around the artwork.

Cut and clean the glass or acrylic. (Chapter 12)

Cut the stiff backing (Chapter 13). If you plan to dry mount or wet mount the artwork to the backing, cut the backing 1" larger in each direction than the mat and glass, and trim it after mounting. If you plan to cover the backing with fabric or provide some other special backing that will be visible behind the artwork, do so at this point.

Cut protective backings if they are to be used between the artwork and the stiff backing. (Chapter 13)

Trim or fold the artwork if necessary (Chapter 9). If you are going to dry mount or wet mount the artwork, you may trim both the artwork and the mounting board to size after mounting.

Attach the artwork to the mat or backing (Chapter 14). If there is no mat and the artwork is the same size as the glass and backing, it is not necessary to attach the artwork as the pressure of the glass will hold it in place.

22 Covering Artwork with Acetate

TOOLS AND MATERIALS
Scissors
Masking tape
*Acetate or mylar — Sold by the roll or by the sheet in art
   supply stores.*

It is available with clear or matte finish in several thicknesses. For covering artwork, use clear acetate or mylar 0.003″ thick. Heavier sheets may be used but they become brittle and tear more easily. Acetate is less expensive but the composition may vary so mylar is preferable for valuable artwork. Purchase a piece at least 6″ longer in each direction than the artwork.

The backing used with acetate is usually corrugated cardboard or Fome-Cor. Mat board may be used in addition to the stiff backing when you want the backing to be a certain color. Mat board is not stiff enough to be used as the only backing except for items less than 12″ x 16″.

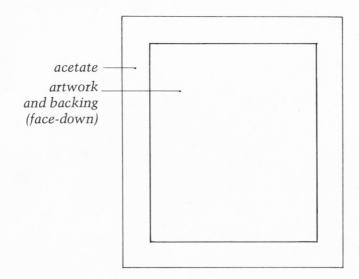

acetate
artwork
and backing
(face-down)

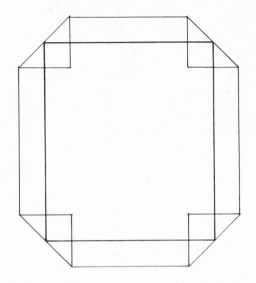

TO COVER THE ARTWORK WITH ACETATE Prepare the materials following the instructions on pp. 180-181.

Cut the acetate 6″ longer in each direction than the backing. Place the acetate on a clean tabletop. The acetate attracts dust easily and any tiny objects on the table will make impressions in its surface.

Place the artwork and backing face-down on the acetate.

Fold the corners of the acetate over as shown and tape them in place. Then fold the sides of the acetate over and tape them to the backing.

Attach cloth or plastic hangers about a third of the way down the back for hanging. (Chapter 33)

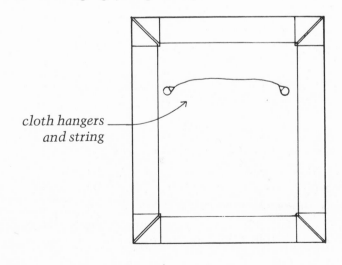

cloth hangers and string

183

23 Clip Frames

THE ESSENTIAL COMPONENTS of a clip frame are glass or acrylic, a stiff backing, and clips. A mat may also be used.

Fome-Cor is generally used as a backing for pieces over 16″ x 20″. Either Fome-Cor or corrugated cardboard can be used for the smaller sizes. Most people prefer the Fome-Cor since it looks nicer on the edge than the cardboard. If you are framing a piece of fabric or needle-work with a clip frame, stretch the fabric on a thin backing such as Fome-Cor, chipboard, or ⅛″ plywood. Stretcher frames and thick backings will not fit into a clip frame.

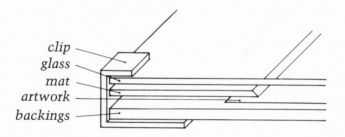

clip
glass
mat
artwork
backings

TO ASSEMBLE A CLIP FRAME:

Prepare the contents of the frame following the instructions on pp. 180-181.

Assemble the contents of the frame — backing, artwork, mat, and glass — face-up on the table. Check the glass to be sure it is clean.

Align the edges and tape the pieces together near each corner so that they will not slip while you are putting the clips on.

Turn the whole package face-down on the table. Place magazines or scraps of mat board underneath it to elevate the edges so that you can reach underneath to attach the clips.

Attach the clips according to the instructions on the package.

A common problem when assembling small clip frames is that

the backing is too thick and won't fit into the clip. If you have this problem:

Remove the backing from the artwork and glass.

Put the clips in place on the backing.

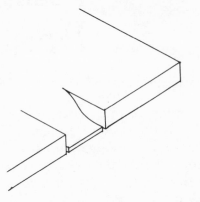

Slit the edge of the backing with a mat knife on either side of each clip.

Remove the clips and pound the edge of the backing flat between the slits.

This will allow the clips to fit into place and the rest of the backing will look normal.

24 Plastic Box Frames

A PLASTIC BOX FRAME consists of a plastic box and a slightly smaller cardboard box that holds the artwork in place. You do not need the usual stiff backing, but you may use protective backings. If you are cutting a mat to fit into a box frame, measure the opening in the back of the box and subtract ¹⁄₁₆″ from each dimension to determine the size of the mat.

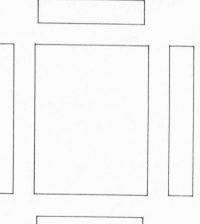

TO BUILD A BOX FRAME:

Prepare the artwork. (Chapter 9)

Cut the mat if you are using one. (Chapter 11)

Cut the acrylic pieces. (Chapter 12) There will be five — the front and the four sides.

The front of the box. The width will be the width of the artwork or mat plus twice the thickness of the acrylic plus ¹⁄₁₆″. The height will be the height of the artwork or mat plus twice the thickness of the acrylic plus ¹⁄₁₆″.

The sides. Decide how deep you want the box to be — about 1″ is standard. The length of the side pieces will be the same as the height of the front, and their width will be the depth of the box.

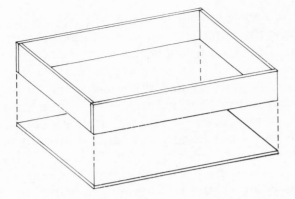

The top and bottom pieces. The length will be the width of the front piece minus twice the thickness of the acrylic. The width will be the same as that of the two side pieces.

File and sand the edges but do not polish them. (Chapter 12) Glue the four sides together as shown. Then glue the sides to the front of the box. Regular glues will not work on acrylic. You must use a solvent that actually fuses the two pieces of acrylic together. Common solvents for acrylic are IPS Weld On #3 Solvent, Methylene Chloride, Ethylene Dichloride, or 1-1-2 Trichlorethane. You can purchase the solvents along with a syringe-type applicator from a plastics dealer.

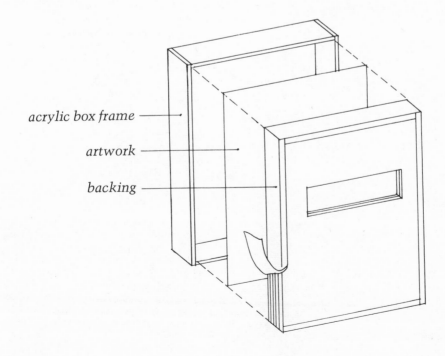

acrylic box frame

artwork

backing

187

Hold the two pieces together with masking tape while you apply the solvent along the outside of the joint. (Capillary action will draw the solvent in.) Take care to apply the solvent only along the crack, since any drops on the surface of the acrylic will leave visible marks. The solvent sets up quickly and the masking tape can be removed about ten minutes after applying the solvent, but handle the work carefully — the joint doesn't reach full strength for several hours.

Build a backing for the box by cutting several pieces of Fome-Cor slightly smaller than the opening in the back of the box. Place the artwork, and mat if you have one, in the box. Stack up as many pieces of Fome-Cor as you need to fill the rest of the box. Bind the edges of the Fome-Cor together with paper tape or cloth. Cut the holes in the last two pieces about one third of the way down from the top so that you can get a fingerhold on the Fome-Cor to pull it out of the box. These holes will also be the support for hanging.

25 Passe-Partout Frames

TOOLS AND MATERIALS
Straightedge
Mat knife or razor blade
Masking tape
Strong cloth, plastic, or paper tape — Because the tape must hold the glass in place, stretchy *plastic tape like electrician's tape is not satisfactory*
Two passe-partout rings — available at a picture frame shop or from Twin City Moulding and Supply — or gummed cloth hangers

The weight of the framing materials is a problem with passe-partout framing, as the tape bears the weight of the glass and the passe-partout hangers can't support heavy items. The backing should be lightweight, preferably Fome-Cor or corrugated cardboard. Acrylic is better than glass as it is much lighter.

You will also need a protective backing between the stiff backing and the artwork because the passe-partout hangers pass through the stiff backing and could scratch the back of the artwork.

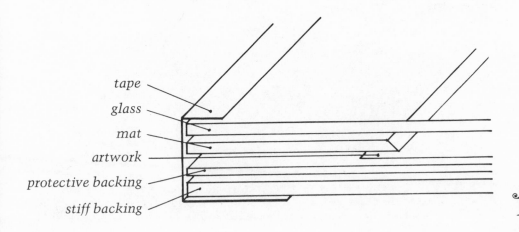

tape
glass
mat
artwork
protective backing
stiff backing

TO ASSEMBLE THE PASSE-PARTOUT FRAME:

Prepare the contents of the frame following the instructions on pp. 180-181.

Slit the stiff backing and insert two passe-partout rings about one third of the way down from the top and about 3″ in from the sides. Open the prongs and tape them in place.

Assemble the contents of the frame — stiff backing, protective backing, artwork, mat, and glass — face-up on the table. Be sure the glass is clean.

Align the edges and temporarily tape the pieces together near each corner with masking tape so that they will stay aligned while you are applying the passe-partout tape.

Move the whole package, still face-up, until one edge extends slightly over the edge of the table. Remove the masking tape along that edge.

Bind the glass to the backing with passe-partout tape. I find that the best way to apply the tape in a straight line is to tape a straight-edge to the front of the glass about ¼″ in from the edge and use it as a guide for placing the tape. Apply the tape to the front of the glass first — it should extend ¼″ or more over the front of the glass. Then smooth it into place along the edge and back of the picture. Trim off the ends even with the edge of the glass.

Tape the opposite side next, then the remaining two sides. Overlap the tape at the corners and trim it even with the edge of the glass.

Run a wire between the passe-partout rings on the back.

Taping a straightedge in place ¼″ in from the edge of the glass.

Applying tape to the front of the glass using the straightedge as a guide.

Completed frame with playbill floated on colored mat board backing.

26 Homemade Metal Frames

TOOLS AND MATERIALS
  Miter box
  Hacksaw
  C-clamp or spring clamp
  Awl
  Screwdriver
  Aluminum counter molding

Homemade metal frames may be used for fabric or paintings on wood stretcher frames, for artwork that has been mounted on a wood backing, or for artwork with glass, mat, and backing. In the latter case an additional wood backing must be inserted to support the metal strips. The wood backing makes this a heavy frame so I recommend using acrylic instead of glass to make the frame as light as possible.

The stripping to use for a homemade metal frame is aluminum counter molding, available at hardware stores in 6-foot lengths with holes already drilled and a packet of screws. It comes in different widths. Stripping ⅞" deep will hold a painting on a standard precut stretcher frame, but not one on a homemade stretcher frame, and it is

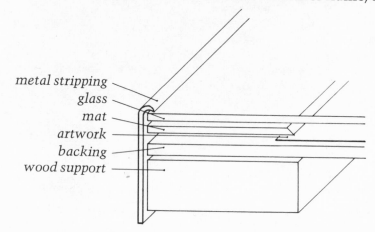

metal stripping
glass
mat
artwork
backing
wood support

not deep enough to accommodate glass, mat, and backing with the necessary wood support. Stripping 1¼″ wide will make a frame deep enough for any of these situations.

When you purchase the stripping look carefully at each piece and make sure they all match. Sometimes they will vary slightly in shape. Metal stripping also scratches easily, so be sure to buy un-scratched lengths and handle it carefully.

Assembling the components of a home-made metal frame.

TO ASSEMBLE THE METAL FRAME:

Prepare the contents of the frame following the instructions on pp. 180-181.

Cut a wood backing (Chapter 13) or build a wood stretcher frame (Chapter 16) to support the metal stripping. This step is not necessary for framing fabric that is already stretched on a wood backing or stretcher frame. If you use a solid plywood backing the usual stiff backing will not be necessary.

Assemble the contents of the frame — wood support, stiff backing, artwork, mat, and glass face-up on the table. Check to be sure the glass is clean. Place scraps of mat board or cardboard under the wood backing so that it is elevated from the tabletop.

Measure along one edge of the artwork to determine the length of the metal strip.

It is essential to secure the stripping to the wood support as often as possible to make the frame tighter and stronger. So when you measure the stripping, include as many screw holes as possible in each length, even if it means wasting a little. Measure the stripping

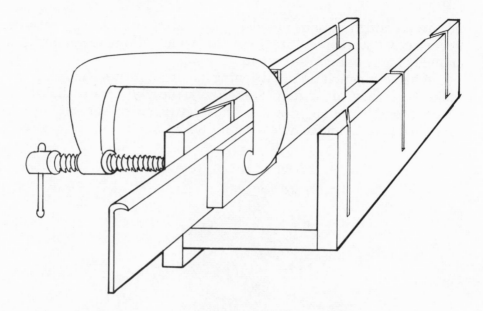

along the inside surface. Mark the cutting line with a pencil and do not add any tolerances: measure and cut the stripping exactly the same length as the artwork.

To cut the metal stripping:

Place the stripping in the miter box in a vertical position face-up. The surface of the metal scratches easily, so don't slide it in the miter box. Place a small block of wood against the inside edge of the stripping to cushion it; then hold it in place with a C-clamp or spring clamp.

Measuring to determine the length of the third and fourth sides of the frame.

Draw the hacksaw slowly toward you across the top surface of the metal to start the cut. Continue to cut with light pressure. Progress will be slow. Be sure to keep the hacksaw in a vertical position—if you slant it to either side the cut will be crooked.

Attach the metal stripping to the wood backing. The lip of the frame should press firmly on the glass or acrylic, or on the front of the artwork, and the metal strip should be centered with each end exactly at the corner. If the bottom edge of the strip is touching the tabletop, elevate the artwork and backing more. Hold the stripping in place, start holes in the wood support with an awl, and then screw the strip into place.

Measure the opposite side next. Cut the metal stripping and attach it. Then measure the remaining two sides and cut the stripping to fit exactly between the two pieces that are already in position. Screw these pieces into place.

27 Wood Frames

PREPARE THE CONTENTS of the frame following the instructions on pp. 180-181.

Build the wood frame as follows:

Clean the finish on an old frame or strip the frame down to the raw wood or steel wool the surface lightly to prepare it for additional coats of finish. (Chapter 18)

Finish raw wood molding or apply additional finish to an old frame if needed (Chapter 19). You can finish the raw molding in one piece or you can cut it to size first and then finish it. Clear finishes should be applied before the corners of the frame are joined, as glue and putty will seal the pores of raw wood and keep the finish from penetrating. Opaque finishes such as paint and metal leaf may be applied before or after joining the corners.

Cut the molding. (Chapter 17)

Join the corners of the frame (Chapter 20). Remember to try the frame around the artwork first and make sure it fits.

Fit the artwork into the frame and seal the back. (Chapter 21)

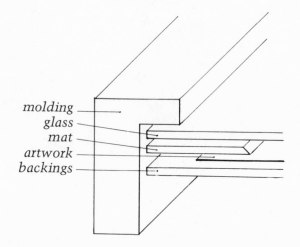

molding
glass
mat
artwork
backings

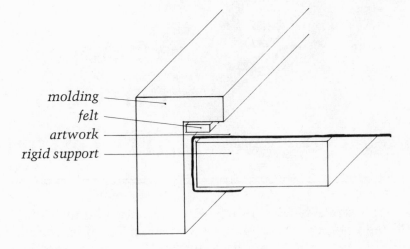

molding

felt

artwork

rigid support

28 Wood Frames with Liners

To BUILD A FRAME with a liner you will need two moldings, one to build the liner, the other to build the frame. The liner molding must fit easily inside the frame molding, so the latter should be deeper. Avoid using moldings with slanting sides for liners, for they are difficult to measure and to secure in place.

Prepare the contents of the frame following the instructions on pp. 180-181.

Build a frame with a liner as follows:

Finish the raw moldings for both the frame and the liner. You can finish the molding in one piece or cut it to size and then finish it. Clear finishes should always be applied before the corners of the frame are joined, as glue and putty will seal the pores of the wood and keep the finish from penetrating. Opaque finishes such as paint and metal leaf may be applied before or after joining the corners. (Chapter 19)

Cut the molding to be used as the liner. (Chapter 17)

Join the corners of the liner. (Chapter 20)

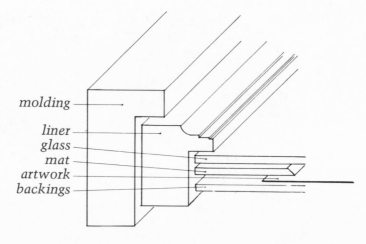

molding
liner
glass
mat
artwork
backings

Measure the liner from outside corner to outside corner and add ⅛" to the measurement to determine the size of the frame.

Cut the molding to be used as the frame. (Chapter 17)

Try the frame pieces around the liner to make sure they fit.

Join the corners of the frame. (Chapter 20)

Fit the liner into place inside the frame. Fasten it in by gluing it or by tacking through it into the inside edge of the frame with wire brads.

Fit the contents of the frame into place. (Chapter 21)

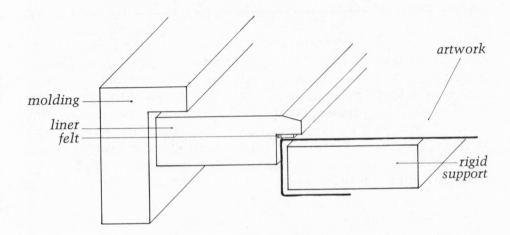

29 Slat Frames

A SLAT FRAME, made from wood stripping, can be used only for artwork on a wood stretcher frame or for artwork that is permanently mounted on a wood backing. It is attached to the artwork by nailing through the frame into the wood backing. The stripping may be cut with mitered or square corners, and the corners are usually not joined. If you glue the corners together and then nail through the stripping into the wood support, it is impossible to remove the frame without destroying it in the process. Glass or acrylic can't be used with a slat frame, as there is no lip to hold it in place.

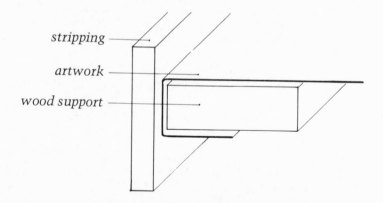

stripping

artwork

wood support

FOR FABRIC, NEEDLEWORK, OR PAINTINGS ON CANVAS

Prepare the contents of the frame as follows:

Iron the fabric to remove fold lines or wrinkles. Do not iron painted fabric, as heat may affect the paint. Block and press needlepoint or embroidery. (Chapter 16)

Stretch the artwork on a solid wood backing or a wood stretcher frame. (Chapter 16)

Measure the stretched piece. (Chapter 10)

FOR ARTWORK ON PAPER

Prepare the contents of the frame as follows:

Remove the artwork from an old frame or mat. Clean or flatten the artwork if necessary. (Chapter 9)

Measure the artwork. (Chapter 10)

Trim the artwork if necessary. (Chapter 9)

Cut the wood backing exactly the size of the artwork (Chapter 13). Sand the edges smooth and paint them black so that no raw wood will be visible from the front of the frame. You can use plywood or particle board, ½" thick or thicker. Both are available at lumberyards. The particle board is made of compressed wood chips and is easier to sand than the plywood.

Mount the artwork to the backing. (Chapter 15)

TO BUILD A SLAT FRAME:

Finish the raw wood (Chapter 19). You can finish it in one piece or cut it and then finish it. Stripping must be finished before it is attached to the artwork. Stripping is commonly painted black on the inside, stained or painted on the outside, and metal-leafed on the front edge. It is also common to paint or stain all the surfaces the same way.

Cut the stripping. For mitered corners, follow the instructions in Chapter 17; if you want square corners cut the top and bottom pieces exactly the width of the artwork, and cut the two side pieces the height of the artwork plus twice the width of the stripping.

Attach the stripping to the artwork. You can place the stripping so that the front edge is flush with the front edge of the artwork or so that the artwork is recessed in the frame.

If you want the front of the stripping to be flush with the front of the artwork, place the artwork face-down on the table with one edge against the wall. Place the piece of stripping face down against the opposite edge of the artwork and center it, lining up the ends of the stripping with the corners of the artwork. Nail the stripping into the side of the wood backing using wire brads 1" or longer. Set the brads just below the surface of the frame and cover them with putty. Attach the rest of the pieces in the same way. Support the artwork against the wall whenever you nail into the backing.

If you want the artwork to be recessed in the frame, place the artwork face-up on the table with the stripping face-up also against the side of the artwork. Nail the stripping into the side of the wood backing as described above.

Seal the back of the frame. (Chapter 21)

30 Floater Frames

THE FLOATER FRAME can be used only for artwork that is either on a wood stretcher frame or permanently mounted on a wood backing. It is attached to the artwork with metal clips that screw into the wood backing. Glass or acrylic can't be used with a floater frame since there is no lip to hold it in place.

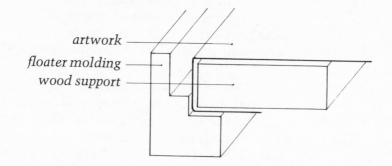

artwork
floater molding
wood support

FOR FRAMING FABRIC, NEEDLEWORK, OR PAINTINGS ON CANVAS

Prepare the contents of the frame as follows:

Iron fabric to remove fold lines or wrinkles. Do not iron painted fabric since the heat may affect the paint.

Block and press needlepoint or crewel embroidery. (Chapter 16)

Stretch the artwork on a solid wood backing or a wood stretcher frame. (Chapter 16)

Measure the stretched piece. (Chapter 10)

FOR FRAMING PAPER ARTWORK

Prepare the contents of the frame as follows:

Remove the artwork from an old frame or mat. Clean or flatten the artwork if necessary. (Chapter 9)

Measure the artwork. (Chapter 10)

Trim the artwork if necessary. (Chapter 9)

Cut the wood backing exactly the size of the artwork (Chapter 13). Sand the edges smooth and paint them black so that no raw wood will be visible from the front of the frame. You can use plywood or particle board, ½" thick or thicker.

Both are available at lumberyards. The particle board is made of compressed wood chips and is easier to sand than the plywood.

Mount the artwork to the backing. (Chapter 15)

TO BUILD A FRAME WITH FLOATER MOLDING

Finish the raw wood (Chapter 19). You can finish it in one piece or cut it and then finish it. Clear finishes must be applied before the corners are joined, as glue and putty will seal the pores of the wood and keep the finish from penetrating. Opaque finishes such as paint or metal leaf may be applied before or after joining the corners of the frame. The inside surfaces of a floater molding are usually painted black to give the illusion that the artwork is floating. The outside of the molding is usually painted or stained. And the front edge is usually painted with a metallic paint or metal leafed.

Cut the molding. (Chapter 17)

Join the corners of the frame (Chapter 20). Before joining the corners, try the frame around the artwork and make sure it fits.

Fit the artwork into the frame and seal the back. (Chapter 21)

31 Building a Shadow Box Frame

THE SHADOW BOX frame has a deep spacer between the glass and the backing to accommodate three-dimensional objects. There are shadow box moldings that have two lips, one for the glass and one for the backing. But these do not come in a wide variety of styles. Most shadow boxes are constructed with a standard wood molding and spacers to separate the glass from the backing.

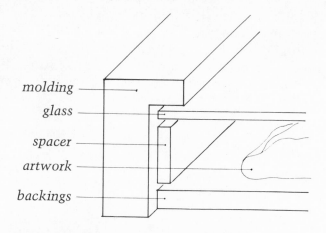

molding

glass

spacer

artwork

backings

TO BUILD A SHADOW BOX FRAME

Cut the stiff backing (Chapter 13). This backing must be rigid enough to support the weight of the object being framed. Since the backing in a shadow box frame is usually visible from the front of the frame, choose a backing the appropriate color and texture, or stain or paint it, cover it with fabric, mount colored paper, or mat board onto the front surface of it. If you stretch cloth on the backing, remeasure it after stretching to determine the size of the frame and glass. (Chapter 15)

Attach the artwork to the backing. (Chapter 14)

Cut and clean the glass or acrylic (Chapter 12). If you are using a standard wood molding cut the glass exactly the same size as the backing. If you are using a shadow box molding with two lips, assemble the frame and then measure the opening to determine what size to cut the glass.

Clean the finish on an old frame or strip the frame down to the raw wood or steel wool the surface lightly to prepare it for additional coats of finish. (Chapter 13)

Finish raw wood molding or apply additional finish to an old frame if needed (Chapter 19). You can finish the raw molding in one piece or you can cut it to size first and then finish it. Clear finishes should be applied before the corners of the frame are joined, as glue and putty will seal the pores of the raw wood and keep the finish from penetrating. Opaque finishes such as paint and metal leaf may be applied before or after joining the corners.

Cut the molding. (Chapter 17)

Join the corners of the frame (Chapter 20). Before you join the corners, try the frame around the artwork to make sure it fits.

Fit the glass into the frame, glue or tack the spacers in place, fit the artwork into the frame, and seal the back. (Chapter 21)

32 Two-sided Frames

THERE ARE TWO COMMON methods of building a two-sided frame. You can use a standard wood molding and fasten the contents of the frame into place with thin strips of wood, or you can place the artwork between two pieces of acrylic and rivet the acrylic together at the corners.

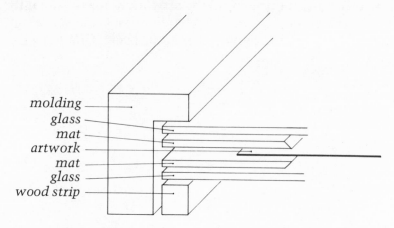

molding
glass
mat
artwork
mat
glass
wood strip

To build a two-sided frame with a wood molding:

Remove the artwork from an old frame or mat. Clean or flatten the artwork if necessary. (Chapter 9)

Measure the artwork. (Chapter 10)

Cut the mats if you are using them (Chapter 11). The outside dimensions of both mats will be the same, but the windows may be different or they may be located differently with respect to the outside of the mat. So cut one mat and temporarily attach the artwork to it. Then place it face-down on the table and measure in from the edges to determine the location of the window for the other mat. If you are planning to paint the mats or cover them with fabric, do that before proceeding. The width of the fabric may add a little to the measurements of the mat, so you will want to remeasure it before cutting the glass or frame. And since it's hard to visualize how a painted mat will look, you may want to cut the outside of the mats a little large to begin with and then trim it to the size you want it after you decorate it and see it around the artwork.

Cut and clean the glass or acrylic (Chapter 12). It is not safe to put glass on both sides of the artwork since the paper could be torn to shreds if both pieces of glass break. Acrylic on one side will afford you the same protection as a stiff backing behind the artwork. For even more protection, use acrylic on both sides.

Trim or fold the artwork if necessary. (Chapter 9)

Attach the artwork to one of the mats (Chapter 14). If you are not using mats, the pressure of the glass will hold the artwork in place.

Old frames are not generally used for two-sided frames since it is difficult to strip old paper and glue from the back without marring the finish on the sides of the frame. But if you are using an old frame, clean the finish or strip the frame down to the raw wood, or steel wool the surface lightly to prepare it for additional coats of finish. (Chapter 18)

Finish raw wood molding or apply additional finish to an old frame if needed (Chapter 19). You can finish the raw molding in one piece or you can cut it to size first and then finish it. Clear finishes should be applied before the corners of the frame are joined, as glue and putty will clog the pores of raw wood and keep the finish from penetrating. Opaque finishes such as paint and metal leaf may be applied before or after joining the corners.

Cut the molding. (Chapter 17)

Join the corners of the frame (Chapter 20). Before you join the corners, try the molding around the glass and mats to make sure it fits.

Fit the artwork into the frame following the instructions for two-sided frames in Chapter 21.

To frame the artwork between two pieces of acrylic:

Cut and clean the acrylic (Chapter 12). The acrylic must be larger than the artwork so that the screw posts don't injure the artwork.

Scrape, sand, and polish the edges of the acrylic. (Chapter 12)

Place the artwork between the pieces of acrylic.

Tape the acrylic together in a few places so it doesn't slip.

Make sure the edges of the acrylic are aligned and clamp them to a stable wood backing such as a work bench or piece of plywood.

Drill a hole near each corner. (Chapter 12)

Fasten the acrylic sheets together with screw posts (these are sometimes called Chicago Screws and are available in stationery stores) or rivets.

Hanging and Displaying Your Artwork

33 Hanging Pictures

THE PICTURE HANGERS sold in hardware stores specify how much weight they can hold, so if your picture is at all heavy, weigh it before you go shopping for hangers. Most hangers are attached to the wall by a thin nail or wire brad, but occasionally you will need a stronger fixture. If your walls are hollow, you can use Toggle Bolts, Molly Bolts, Hollow Wall Anchors, or Hollow Wall Drive Fasteners. All of these open up inside the wall so that they can't fall out. You must drill a hole in the wall to insert them.

If you have masonry walls, use Vinyl Screw Anchors or Lead Screw Shields for heavyweight pictures. You must drill to insert these, too. For lightweight frames, you can hammer a carbon nail into masonry.

SCREW EYES AND WIRE Several sizes of screw eyes are available. Choose the largest one you think you can use without splitting the molding. Generally, #217½ should be used in very small (less than ½" wide) moldings, and #212 or 210½ is about right for large moldings or wooden stretchers. When you purchase the screw eyes, look at the shaft and be sure it isn't so long that it will come out the other side of the molding. There are screw eyes available with short shafts and these are better for framing.

The best wire for hanging pictures is braided picture wire. It comes in several weights and is available in hardware stores.

Put the screw eyes into the center of the molding (if you are framing fabric on stretcher frame, put them into the stretcher frame instead) about a third of the way down from the top of the frame. If the screw eye is too close to either edge of the molding, the wood may split. Start the hole for the screw eye with an awl or nail. Put the screw into the frame as far as it will go using the awl to turn it. If splitting may be a problem, lubricate the screw eye first with some soap or candle wax.

Attach the wire by sticking it through the screw eye and then

Looping the wire through the screw eye so it won't slip out.

looping it back through again. This keeps it from slipping out. Wrap off the end of the wire by twisting it around the main wire.

Leave about 1" slack in the wire. If the wire is too loose, the top of the frame will hang out from the wall.

Large or heavy frames should have 6 screw eyes placed in the frame in the positions shown. Attach the wire to one screw eye at

Attaching the wire to the back of a large frame using six screw eyes.

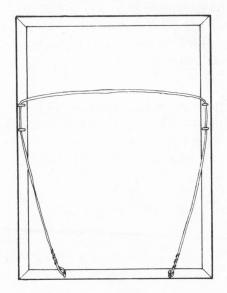

the bottom of the frame. Run it up that side of the frame, through the screw eyes on the side, across, and through the screw eyes on the other side; attach it to the screw eye on the bottom of the frame at the other side as shown. The wire is not attached to the screw eyes on the sides — it only runs through them. This arrangement distributes the weight and actually pulls the frame together when you hang it.

OTHER HANGING DEVICES

Sawtooth hangers   These are small metal pieces which can be tacked into the top of the frame to hang small or lightweight pictures. You can put one in the middle at the top or one at each top corner. The sawtooth edge rests on a nail on the wall. Sawtooth hangers can be purchased at hardware stores.

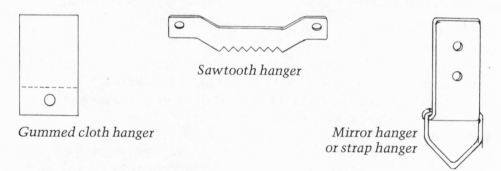

Sawtooth hanger

Gummed cloth hanger

Mirror hanger or strap hanger

Mirror hangers or strap hangers   This is an alternative method for hanging heavy pictures framed in a large molding. Screw the hanger into the molding about a third of the way down from the top of the frame. Use heavyweight braided picture wire and attach it as you would with ordinary screw eyes. These hangers are available at hardware stores.

Cloth hangers or gummed plastic hangers   These are also called Bull Dog Picture Hanging Eyes. They are good for hanging very lightweight pictures, posters dry mounted on foam board, or artwork covered with acetate or just matted. Attach them to the backing about a third of the way down from the top, one near each side. Run a piece of string between them. They can be purchased at some dimestores and hardware stores and from frame stores.

212   **TIPS FOR HANGING PICTURES**   Instead of putting only one nail or picture hook in the wall, put in two about as far apart as half the width of the molding. This distributes the weight of the picture and makes it easier to keep the frame straight on the wall.

If your room has ceiling molding you can hang pictures with molding hooks and long wires instead of nailing into the wall.

Shoulder hooks or square screw hooks are often used to hang passe-partout frames or pictures with only glass, mat, and backing. These little L-shaped pieces screw into the wall and the L-shaped end holds the glass in place. Hooks may be placed on all four sides or on the two sides and the bottom. Before you try this method, make sure your walls will hold a screw.

Many framers put little cork or felt pads on the back of the frame at the bottom corners to hold the bottom of the picture out from the wall so that the top doesn't hang out further than the bottom. They also allow air circulation behind the frame. Adhesive-backed felt can be purchased in dimestores. Just cut it and stick it onto your frame.

There are also self-sticking rubber bumpers made for furniture. These are available in some hardware stores.

34 A Simple Stand for Frames

IF YOU PREFER to set your framed picture on a mantel or tabletop you have two choices. You can look for easel backs — these are hard to find and come only in a few standard sizes, but some frame shops and picture frame suppliers have them. Or you can make a fabric-covered cardboard easel yourself.

To do this, cut a piece of corrugated cardboard the same size as the backing in the frame. We will also call this piece the backing.

Cut another piece of cardboard like the one shown in the drawing. We will call this part the stand.

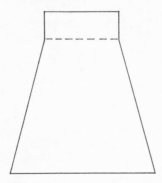

Cut partway through the stand on the dotted line. Label that side front and the other side back.

Cut a length of ribbon to run between the backing and the stand.

Cut a slit the same width as the ribbon through the easel about a third of the way up from the bottom. Thread one end of the ribbon through the easel and glue it to the back.

Cover one side of the backing and the back of the stand with fabric. To do this, cut the fabric a little larger than the cardboard. Pull the edges of the fabric around the cardboard and glue them in place .

Cut a slit through the backing about a third of the way up from the bottom. Thread the other end of the ribbon through the slit and glue it to the cardboard on the other side.

214

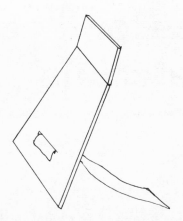

Place the stand flat against the backing and line up the bottom edges. Glue or sew the top portion of the easel to the backing.

Fasten the easel into the back of the frame with brads or turn buttons. (Chapter 21)

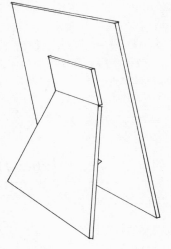

Sources for Tools and Materials

Charrette
Mail Order Department
2000 Mass. Ave.
Cambridge, Mass. 02140
   Art and architectural supplies including high-quality drawing and cutting instruments and colored papers. They will send a catalog on request.

Eubank Frame, Inc.
P.O. Box 425
Salisbury, Maryland 21801
   Suppliers for Eubank Frame and Uni-Frames. They will refer you to retail outlets near you where you can buy their products, or they will ship to you directly if there is no retailer in your area.

Kulicke
636 Broadway
New York, N.Y. 10012
   Supplier for the Kulicke Metal Section Frame, Box Frame, Strip Frame, and others. You can mail-order from them or look for their products in a local frame store or gallery.

Talas
Division of Technical Library Service
104 Fifth Ave.
New York, N.Y. 10011
   Talas is a supplier of tools and materials for bookbinding and art restoration. They carry many archival materials including white or colored all-rag papers, decorated book papers, acid-free tissue paper, and archival glues. Their catalog costs $1.

Twin City Moulding and Supply
2505 University Ave.
St. Paul, Minn. 55114
   Supplier for framing tools and hardware, Braquettes, Fast Frames, and Framekits. They will send a catalog on request.